Tipsy Smoothies

Over 150 Fabulous Cocktail Smoothie Recipes

Donna Pliner Rodnitzky

THREE RIVERS PRESS

NEW YORK

Published by Three Rivers Press. Member of the Crown Publishing Group, a division of Random House, Inc., New York.

Three Rivers Press is a registered trademark and the Three Rivers Press colophon is a trademark of Random House, Inc.

Random House, Inc., has designed this book to provide information in regard to the subject matter covered. It is sold with the understanding that the publisher and the author are not liable for the misconception or misuse of information provided. Every effort has been made to make this book as complete and as accurate as possible. The author and Random House, Inc., shall have neither liability nor responsibility to any person or entity with respect to any loss, damage, or injury caused or alleged to be caused directly or indirectly by the information contained in this book.

Printed in the United States of America

Interior illustrations by Kate Vasseur

Library of Congress Cataloging-in-Publication Data
Rodnitzky, Donna.
    Tipsy smoothies : over 150 fabulous cocktail smoothie recipes / Donna Pliner Rodnitzky
        p.   cm.
    Includes index.
    ISBN 0-7615-2650-1
    1. Cocktails. 2. Smoothies (Beverages). I. Title.
TX951.R653   2003
641.8'72—dc21   2002156423

10 9 8 7 6 5 4 3 2 1

First Edition

Visit us online at www.randomhouse.com

With affection and gratitude to my husband, Bob, who has made it possible for me to pursue my career as a cookbook writer. Without his enthusiastic and generous encouragement in all my endeavors, Tipsy Smoothies *and my other books may never have come to fruition. As always, my children, David, Adam, and Laura, continue to be a source of pride for me. I admire them for their perseverance and dedication to excellence.*

Acknowledgments

I give my heartfelt thanks to Prima Publishing, especially Denise Sternad, acquisitions editor, for putting her trust in me to write this book. Words simply aren't adequate to express my gratitude to Michelle McCormack for being a superb and supportive editor and an absolute joy to work with these past years. Finally, my thanks go to cover designer Monica Thomas and to the entire staff at Prima Publishing for their excellent professionalism in bringing this book to publication.

Introduction

*Candy is dandy
but liquor is quicker.*

—OGDEN NASH

The art of mixing drinks, currently among the most celebrated trends, is nothing new. Cocktails were on our ancestors' menus since early civilization. Some claim that the first cocktail prepared was a combination of lemon juice and powdered vipers. While that one may not sound enticing, mixed drinks have been enjoyed by diverse societies for thousands of years. Today, with the great variety of cocktail ingredients available and modern combinations such as those presented in this book, there is a stimulating libation to suit every person's palate, whether or not he or she has a taste for pulverized snakes.

The origin of the word *cocktail* remains a mystery, and its actual beginning may never be known. There are, however, a few accounts that are both amusing and interesting. The French maintain the cocktail was their invention because, in the early eighteenth century, people in the Bordeaux area drank a blend of Champagne and brandy called the *coquetel*. On the other hand, the 1806 edition of the American magazine *The Balance* states: "Cocktail is a stimulating liquor, composed of spirits of any kind, sugar, water, and bitters—it is vulgarly called bittered sling and is supposed to be an excellent electioneering potion."

Another legend dates back to the beginning of the 1800s, when there was fighting between the southern states and the young King Axolot VIII of Mexico. When the two sides finally made peace, arrangements were made for the American general to meet with the king in his tent and enjoy a reconciling drink. An attractive young woman entered the tent carrying an emerald-ornamented gold cup with an unusual drink she had created. However, because she had only one cup, either the King or the general would have had to drink first, which would have been an embarrassment to the other. The astute woman resolved the dilemma by drinking the cup herself. The general asked the king about this woman, and he replied that she was his daughter Coctel. The general thereupon bowed to the king, and pronounced: "Coctel shall be famous in my country and all over the world. Her name shall never be forgotten."

Although we may never learn the true origin of the word *cocktail*, we do know that the rise in popularity of mixed drinks in America occurred during the Prohibition years. During this time, it was common for illegal bars to mix special drinks containing a variety of ingredients in order to hide their contraband alcohol content. Long after the days of speakeasies and clubs frequented by flappers and their male admirers, mixing and drinking cocktails has become customary in our modern lifestyle. The classic Martini and trendy Cosmopolitan are examples of cocktails with the staying power to survive decades. Other popular drinks, such as Margaritas, Brandy Alexanders, and Pina Coladas are mainstays on most restaurant menus; and as you will discover in this book, they easily morph into smoothies that are a snap to whip up in your own kitchen or bar.

What makes smoothies all the rage is that these mellow concoctions are made from a simple union of fruit and fruit juice, resulting in a delightful combination that is easily prepared and tastes great. Because many traditional smoothie ingredients mix well with a variety of spirits usually reserved for cocktails, it's only fitting that a cocktail smoothie should become the ultimate way to enjoy these two trendsetters. Bolstered with your favorite alcoholic libation, smoothie cocktails acquire a delectable taste that lingers long after the last sip or strawful. And these wonderful creations, accented with an edible garnish, can be enjoyed as a novel pre-meal cocktail or grace an elegant dessert plate as the grand finale to a candlelight dinner.

Tipsy Smoothies appropriately begins with a chapter entitled "Gathering the Goods: How to Select, Prepare, and Store Fresh Fruit." In this section, you will discover the secrets of selecting and preparing the best fruits for the ultimate tipsy smoothie. Chapter 2, "Shaken, But Not Stirred: Equipment, Techniques, and Glassware for Making Tipsy Smoothies" will prove useful in helping you become familiar with the essential tools and glassware you'll need to transform your kitchen into a mixologist's showcase. You will also find a host of techniques that will enable you to elevate every cocktail smoothie you prepare to the pinnacle of smoothiedom. To hone your skills at welcoming friends with a clink of smoothie glasses, chapter 3, "Toasting—An Unforgettable Art," will prime you with a unique variety of traditional toasts from countries all over the world.

Each of the eight chapters that follow is devoted to a specific spirit ingredient used to make a smoothie cocktail. For example, you'll be delighted to find over 20 recipes in chapter 4 concentrating on tipsy smoothies made with gin. Some, such as the *Singapore Sling Smoothie,* may already be favorites of yours; other new creations, like the surprisingly delectable *Hawaiian Martini Smoothie,* are destined for star status. The ensuing chapters are comprised of recipes calling for rum, vodka, tequila, whiskey, liqueur, brandy, as well as champagne, Asti Spumante, sparkling wine, and similar spirits—totaling over 130 delectable delights. Finally, chapter 12, "Garnishes for Tipsy Smoothies," contains recipes for edible, ornamental garnishes that will enable you to achieve a visually striking presentation as you serve your favorite tipsy smoothie creations.

Once considered only a simple combination of fruit and fruit juice, the basic smoothie has evolved to include sophisticated and sublimely spirited drinks, such as those featured in this book. Whether you experience your first tipsy smoothie on the patio or at a black tie event, you're due for some excitement in a glass.

NATIONAL DRINK HOLIDAYS

That's the Spirit (thatsthespirit.com) provides a list of holidays you probably never knew existed. Mark these on your calendar and give yourself a reason to celebrate!

✦

January 19 ~ Champagne Day

January 31 ~ National Brandy Alexander Day

February 22 ~ National Margarita Day

February 27 ~ National Kahlúa Day

June 19 ~ National Martini Day

July 10 ~ National Piña Colada Day

July 19 ~ National Daiquiri Day

July 27 ~ National Scotch Day

August 16 ~ National Rum Day

October 14 ~ National Vodka Day

October 16 ~ National Liqueur Day

November 8 ~ National Harvey Wallbanger Day

CHAPTER 1

Gathering the Goods

How to Select, Prepare, and Store Fresh Fruit

+

*There is greater relish for the
earliest fruit of the season.*

—MARCUS VALERIUS MARTIALIS,
Roman poet

Fresh fruit is an extremely important compo-
nent of a smoothie, and you'll find it worth
your effort to select the freshest fruit available.
In your mission to create the perfect tipsy
smoothie, you'll want to be well informed about
the wide variety of orchard bounty from which
you can choose. The objective of this chapter is
to acquaint you with these delectable bundles of

flavor and guide you in choosing, storing, and preparing them. To begin with, you should realize that looks can be deceiving when you're choosing fruit that is smoothie-ready; therefore, it's important that you do *not* base your choice on appearance alone. At first glance, a peach may look ripe because of its rich color; however, a number of other less obvious attributes are equally important. You should also attempt to determine whether the fruit has a fresh aroma, how heavy or dense it is, and whether it is firm yet resilient to the touch. These characteristics are often more important than the fruit's color. The good news is that once you become a fruit connoisseur, you will find that determining whether fruit is ripe or not is quite easy.

I am certain that as you become more familiar with the wide array of fruit available, you will delight in making this new generation of deliciously enticing cocktail smoothies. As you navigate the aisles of your favorite farmer's market or produce department, the following information will be useful in your quest for the best nature has to offer.

APPLE

Apples are believed to have originated in Central Asia and Caucasus, but they have been cultivated since prehistoric times. They were brought to the United States at the beginning of the seventeenth century and later to Africa and Australia. Today, there are over 100 varieties of apples commercially grown in the United States.

Apples—whether red, green, or yellow—all have a firm, crisp flesh. Some apples have a sweet flavor with a hint of tartness, while others are less sweet and more tart. Most apples are delicious when made into a smoothie, but your flavor preference will determine the best variety for you.

Selection

When choosing an apple, look for one that is firm and crisp with a smooth and tight skin. Most important, the apple should have a sweet-smelling aroma. Avoid any apple that has a bruised or blemished skin. Another consideration when choosing apples is to buy the organic variety whenever possible. Most nonorganic apples are heavily sprayed with pesticides and later waxed to preserve them and keep them looking fresh. Because organic apples have not been subjected to this treatment, you might find a worm in some of them. These unwelcome visitors can be removed when the apple is cut, thereby removing any health or aesthetic concerns. Wash all apples in cool water and dry well, whether organic or not. You can store apples in the crisper bin of the refrigerator for up to six weeks if they are kept separate from other fruits and vegetables.

APRICOT

The apricot is a round or oblong fruit measuring about two inches in diameter with skin and flesh that are both golden orange in color. It is a very sweet and juicy fruit with a single smooth stone.

The apricot is native to North China and was known to be a food source as early as 2200 B.C.

Selection

When choosing apricots, look for those that are well colored, plump, and fairly firm but yield slightly when gently pressed. Avoid any that are green or yellow in color because this may indicate they are not yet ripe. An apricot that is soft to the touch and juicy is fully ripe and should be eaten right away. If an apricot is hard, it can be placed in a brown paper bag and allowed to ripen at room temperature for a day or two. When an apple or tomato is placed in the same bag, *ethylene*, a colorless gas, is released from the companion fruits and helps the banana to ripen even faster. Once apricots are ripe, you can refrigerate them in the crisper bin of the refrigerator for up to a week. Wash them in cool water just before using.

BANANA

The banana has been around for so long that, according to Hindu legend, it was actually the forbidden fruit of the Garden of Eden. It also is believed that the banana was widely cultivated throughout Asia and Oceania before recorded history and that the Spanish colonists introduced banana shoots to the New World in 1516.

Selection

Bananas are picked when they are green and sweeten as they ripen. When choosing a banana, look for one that is completely yellow. The riper a banana, or the more yellow its skin, the sweeter it is. Bananas that are yellow but have green tips and green necks, or are all yellow except for light green necks, also are ready to eat. Green bananas will ripen at room temperature in two or three days. Alternatively, they can be placed in a brown paper bag to ripen (with an apple or tomato to quicken the ripening process). Once ripe, bananas can be stored at room temperature or in the refrigerator for a couple of days.

BLACKBERRY

The blackberry is a small black, blue, or dark red berry that grows on thorny bushes (brambles). These berries are oblong in shape and grow up to one inch in length. The United States is the world's dominant producer of blackberries. Blackberries are at their peak in flavor and availability from June through September, but may still be found in some supermarkets from November on into April.

Selection

When choosing blackberries, look for ones that are plump and solid with full color and a bright, fresh appearance. Place them in a shallow container to prevent the berries on top from crushing those on the bottom. Cover the container and store it in the crisper bin of the refrigerator for one to two days. Wash blackberries in cool water just before using.

BLUEBERRY

Native to North America, the blueberry has the distinction of being the second most popular berry in the United States. It has been around for thousands of years, but was not cultivated until the turn of the century. Today, 95 percent of the world's commercial crop of blueberries is grown in the United States. Blueberries are at their peak in flavor from mid-April to late September. They are available in the southern states first and gradually move north as the season progresses.

Selection

When choosing blueberries, look for those that are plump and firm with a dark blue color and a silvery "bloom" (the powder on blueberries protects them from the sun . . . it does not rinse off). Avoid any that appear to be dull because this may indicate that the fruit is old. Blueberries should be prepared in the same way as blackberries; however, they can be stored for a longer time in the crisper bin of the refrigerator, from three to five days.

CHERRY

A cherry is a small, round, red to black fruit that grows on a tree. There are numerous varieties, each of which falls into one of three categories: sweet, sour, or a hybrid of the two. Cherries grow in the temperate zones of Europe, Asia, and the Americas. It is believed that they originated in northeastern Asia and later spread throughout the temperate zones in prehistory, carried by birds who ate the cherries and later dropped the stones. Cherries are available from late May through early August.

Selection

When choosing cherries, look for those that are dark red, plump, and firm, and have an attached stem. Store them in the crisper bin of the refrigerator for up to two days and wash them in cool water just before using.

GRAPEFRUIT

The first seedless grapefruit (eight seeds or less) was developed in Florida in the 1800s, followed by the first pink seedless grapefruit in 1913. In the early 1920s, seedless grapefruit began to be cultivated in the richly subtropical Rio Grande Valley in southern Texas. In 1929, the Ruby Red Grapefruit was discovered in the Rio Grande Valley. It was renowned for its deep ruby red color, exceptionally sweet flavor, and superior quality. Today, most grapefruits are cultivated in Texas and Florida, with such varieties as Ruby Red and Star Red from Texas and Indian River and Orchid Island from Florida.

Grapefruits grow in clusters that hang from trees with glossy dark green leaves. Because they are clustered, they resemble grapes, except that they are much larger. The three main varieties are the white, pink/red, and Star Ruby/Rio Red. All grapefruits have a similar tangy-sweet flavor and are exceptionally juicy.

Selection

When selecting a grapefruit, look for one that is round, heavy for its size, springy to the touch, has a skin that is smooth and firm, and exudes a lovely sweet fragrance. Avoid puffy or bruised grapefruit. Wash each one and store it in the crisper bin of the refrigerator for up to six weeks.

MANGO

Mangoes were cultivated in India and the Malay Archipelago as long as four thousand years ago. In the 1700s and 1800s, European explorers introduced the fruit to other tropical areas. Mangoes were first raised in the United States sometime in the early 1900s.

The mango resembles a peach in appearance but is more elongated in shape and generally larger in size. It has a thin, leathery skin that is waxy and smooth and its color can be green, red, orange, yellow, or any combination of those colors. The skin surrounds a very aromatic and juicy pulp and a hard inner pit.

Selection

When choosing a mango, look for one that is very fragrant and plump around the stem area, and gives slightly when pressed. No matter what the color of the mango, the best-flavored ones will have a yellow tinge when ripe. Mangoes also can be ripened at room temperature. To accelerate the process, place the mango and an apple in a brown paper bag and leave on the kitchen counter overnight. Once ripened, it can be stored in the crisper bin of the refrigerator for up to five days. Wash in cool water and dry the fruit well just before using.

MELON

Melons, surprisingly, are members of the cucumber family. They grow on vines that can be up to seven feet long. There are two distinct types of melons: muskmelons and watermelons. The muskmelon category includes summer melons (cantaloupe and muskmelon) and winter melons (casaba and honeydew).

Selection

When choosing a melon, look for one that is unblemished, firm, and free of any soft spots. Pick up a few melons and choose the one that is the heaviest for its size. Also, smell the stem end of the melon to see whether it has a fresh melon aroma. If it has no aroma, then the fruit is not ripe. To ripen a melon, place it in a loosely closed brown paper bag. To speed up this process, add a banana or an apple to the bag. Melons should be washed in cool water and refrigerated until ready to use.

ORANGE

Fresh oranges are widely grown in Florida, California, and Arizona, and are available all year long. The two major varieties are the Valencia and the Navel. Two other varieties grown in the Western states are the Cara Cara and the Moro orange (similar to the blood orange), both of which are available throughout the winter months.

Selection

When selecting an orange, look for one that is heavy for its size and firm. Avoid oranges with bruised skin, indicating possible fermentation, as well as those with loose skin, suggesting they may be dry inside. Although oranges can be stored at room temperature for a few days, their flavor is best when they are kept refrigerated. Wash oranges in cool water before storing them in the crisper bin of the refrigerator.

PAPAYA

The papaya is native to North America and is cultivated in semitropical zones. It grows on trees that can reach heights of twenty feet, and the papaya itself can weigh from one to twenty pounds. The most common variety grown in the United States is the Solo, which flourishes in Hawaii and Florida. This pear-shaped fruit can weigh up to two pounds and is about six inches long. When ripe, the papaya has a distinctive golden-yellow skin. Its flesh, which is similar to its skin in color, is quite juicy and has a wonderful sweet-tart flavor. The center of the papaya is filled with dark, peppery seeds that are edible, but most people prefer to discard them.

Selection

When choosing a papaya, look for one that is richly yellow colored with a smooth, unblemished skin; emits a soft, fruity aroma; and gives slightly to palm pressure. It should also be heavy and symmetrical in size. Avoid any with dark spots. A green papaya will ripen in two to three days at room temperature if placed in a brown paper bag. To accelerate the process, place the papaya in the bag along with an apple or banana. However, be sure to keep those fruits away when the papaya is fully ripe. To store papayas, refrigerate completely ripe ones for up to one week.

PEACH

Grown since prehistoric times, peaches were first cultivated in China. They were later introduced into Europe and Persia. It is believed that the Spaniards brought peaches to North, Central, and South America. The Spanish missionaries planted the first peach trees in California.

Numerous varieties of peaches are available, and they are broken down into rough classifications. One type of peach is the "freestone," so named because the pit separates easily from the peach. Another variety is the "clingstone," in which the pit is firmly attached to the fruit.

The freestone is the peach most often found in supermarkets because it is easy to eat, while clingstones are frequently canned.

Selection

When picking peaches, look for ones that are relatively firm with a fuzzy, creamy yellow skin and a sweet aroma. The pink blush on the peach indicates its variety, not its ripeness. Avoid peaches with wrinkled skin or those that are soft or blemished. The peach should yield gently when touched. To ripen peaches, keep them at room temperature and out of direct sun until the skin yields slightly to the touch. Once they ripen, store them in a single layer in the crisper bin of the refrigerator for up to five days. Wash peaches in cool water just before using.

PEAR

Pear is the name of a tree in the rose family and its fruit. It is believed that pears were eaten by Stone Age people; however, the pears we are accustomed to eating were first cultivated in southeastern Europe and western Asia as "recently" as 2000 B.C. Pear trees were introduced to the Americas when European settlers arrived in the 1700s.

Selection

Pears are a unique fruit because they ripen best *off* the tree, which explains why they are often so hard when purchased at the supermarket. Many pears have stickers that tell you the stage of ripeness, such as "Ready to Eat" or "Let me ripen for two days." When choosing pears, look for ones that are firm and unblemished with a fresh pear aroma. To ripen pears, place them in a brown paper bag at room temperature for a few days. To "kick start" the ripening process, place the pear in a brown paper bag with a ripe banana or an apple. When they yield to gentle thumb pressure, pears are ready to eat. Once ripe, wash pears in cool water and store them in the crisper bin of the refrigerator for two to five days.

PINEAPPLE

The pineapple is a tropical fruit that is native to Central and South America. In 1493, Christopher Columbus discovered pineapples growing on the island of Guadeloupe in the Caribbean and brought them back to Spain. By the 1700s, pineapples were being grown in greenhouses throughout Europe.

Selection

When choosing a pineapple, look for one that has a fresh pineapple aroma and a crown with crisp, fresh-looking green leaves and a brightly colored shell. It should also be heavy and symmetrical in size. Avoid any pineapples that have soft spots or are discolored. To store a pineapple, cut the fruit from the shell and refrigerate it in an airtight container for up to one week.

RASPBERRY

It is believed that red raspberries spread all over Europe and Asia in prehistoric times. Because they were so delicious growing wild, it was not until the 1600s that raspberries were cultivated in Europe. Those that are cultivated in North America originated from two groups: the red raspberry, native to Europe, and the wild red variety, native to North America.

Selection

When choosing raspberries, it is always best to buy them when they are in season—usually starting in late June and lasting four to six weeks. If you are fortunate enough to have a local berry farm, take advantage of it by visiting at the beginning of the season to get the best pick. Select berries that are large and plump, bright, shiny, uniform in color, and free of mold. Avoid any that are mushy. Before refrigerating raspberries, carefully go through the batch and discard any that show signs of spoilage. Place the raspberries in a shallow container to prevent the berries on top from crushing those on the bottom. Cover the container and store it in the crisper bin of the refrigerator for one to two days. Wash raspberries in cool water just before you are ready to use them.

STRAWBERRY

Strawberries date as far back as 2,200 years ago. They are known to have grown wild in Italy in the third century, and by 1588 the first European settlers discovered them in Virginia. Local Indians cultivated the strawberry as early as the mid-1600s and by the middle of the nineteenth century, this fruit was widely grown in many parts of North America.

The strawberry grows in groups of three on the stem of a plant that is very low to the ground. As the fruit ripens, it changes from greenish white in color to a lush, flame red. The strawberry does not have a skin but is actually covered by hundreds of tiny seeds.

Selection

The best time to buy strawberries is in June and July when they are at their peak of juicy freshness. As with raspberries, if you are lucky enough to live near a strawberry farm, a "pick your own" day trip is a wonderful family outing as well as an excellent way to get the very best of the crop. Look for plump, firm, and deep-colored fruit with a bright green cap and a sweet strawberry aroma. Strawberries can be stored in a single layer in the crisper bin of the refrigerator for up to two days. Wash them with their caps in cool water just before you are ready to use them.

FREEZING FRUIT

To make a tipsy smoothie with the optimal consistency, it is important that the fresh fruit you use has been frozen for 30 minutes or more. Using frozen fruit also helps maintain your smoothie at an ideal icy cold temperature. Another reason you may want to freeze fruit is simply to store it for later use. This is especially useful when you know that certain seasonal fruits will no longer be available after a certain date. By purchasing an ample quantity to freeze, you can be certain of having a supply on hand when you need it to prepare one of your favorite smoothies. Also, there may be times when already ripened fruit isn't needed immediately, so freezing prevents over-ripening and allows it to be utilized at a later time.

Whether you are freezing for immediate use or for storage, the basic preparation is identical. Here are specifics for preparing various types of fruit for freezing:

Tips for Freezing Various Fruit Types

- When ready to freeze cherries and apricots (which should be cut in half and their stones removed) or berries, place them in a colander and rinse with a gentle stream of cool water. Pat them dry with a paper towel.

- To freeze a peach, remove its stone and cut it into small pieces.

- To freeze a pear, remove its stem and seeds, and cut it into small pieces.

- For a banana, remove its skin and either slice it or freeze it whole and then slice it later, before use.

- Before freezing oranges and grapefruit, remove the peel and pith, break each into segments, and remove any seeds.

- To prepare apples, mangoes, melons, and papayas for freezing, remove their peels and seeds or pits before cubing.

- When ready to freeze a pineapple, remove its top, the outer layering, and the core, then cut into cubes.

Place prepared fruit on a baking sheet lined with freezer paper, plastic-coated side facing up. In a pinch, you can use waxed paper or parchment paper instead. Freeze the fruit for 30 minutes or longer, after which time it will be ready to add to the other smoothie ingredients. If frozen fruit is to be used at a later date, transfer the frozen pieces to an airtight plastic bag large enough to hold them in a single layer. Label and mark the date on the bag, and freeze for up to two weeks. Most fruit can be kept in the freezer this long without any loss of flavor.

HOW MUCH FRUIT SHOULD I BUY?

To determine how much fruit you need to make a tipsy smoothie, the list below provides an estimate of the quantity of fruit you would get once the skin, hull, seeds, pit, and core are removed. You can use the average weight per individual fruit provided in the table; or, to be more precise, you can weigh the fruit, using the supermarket scale, before purchase.

FRESH FRUIT YIELDS

Fruit	How Much to Buy	Average Weight	Number of Cups
Apple	1 medium	6 ounces	1 cup
Apricots	3	8 ounces	1 cup
Banana	1 large	10 ounces	1 cup
Blackberries	½ pint	6 ounces	1¼ cups
Blueberries	½ pint	8 ounces	1 cup
Cantaloupe	1 medium	3 pounds	5 cups
Cherries	19 to 20	8 ounces	1 cup
Grapefruit	1 medium	12 ounces	1½ cups
Mango	1 medium	10 ounces	1 cup
Orange	1 medium	10 ounces	1 cup
Papaya	1 medium	10 ounces	1 cup
Peach	1 medium	8 ounces	1 cup
Pear	1 medium	6 ounces	1 cup
Pineapple	1 medium	3 pounds	5½ cups
Raspberries	1 box	6 ounces	1¼ cups
Strawberries	7 to 8 medium	6 ounces	1 cup

CHAPTER 2

Shaken, But Not Stirred

Equipment, Techniques, and Glassware
for Making Tipsy Smoothies

✦

*Warning of the century: "Do not
place this Wine Brick in a one-
gallon crock, add sugar and
water, cover and let stand for
seven days, or else an illegal
alcoholic beverage will result."*

—Label from a Prohibition-era product
made of compressed grapes

When thinking about the kind of equipment
needed to prepare mixed drinks, the first
image that comes to mind is that of a cocktail
shaker, the most important item used to make a

classic Martini. What follows immediately are visions of double-ended jiggers, stirrers, strainers, and an assortment of other gadgets. The good news is that to make a tipsy smoothie, it isn't necessary to have an extensive array of equipment. In fact, all you need to outfit your tipsy smoothie bar is a modest number of essential tools: a sharp knife for prepping fruit; measuring spoons and cups; a rubber spatula to remove every last drop from the blender; airtight freezer bags for storing freshly cut fruit in the freezer; and, of course, the essential blender.

There are, in addition, a few optional items of equipment you might want to consider. As you glance through the garnish recipes found in this cookbook, you will note that some of them suggest using a *silicone mat,* a reusable laminated food grade silicone sheet that prevents food from sticking during the baking process. This is a very useful item, but not a necessity. Finally, although a food processor can be used to make a tipsy smoothie, most smoothie experts would agree that a blender is definitely the preferred appliance. You can use a food processor to purée fruit and ice, but it often leaves small chunks of ice, while a blender breaks up the ice and fruit into tiny particles and is better able to process liquids and solids into a fine, smooth, and well-aerated purée.

EQUIPMENT

The blender is by far the most important piece of kitchen equipment you will need to make a proper smoothie. The invention of this indispensable appliance is credited to Stephen J. Poplawski who, in 1922, first conceived placing a spinning blade at the bottom of a glass container. By 1935, Fred Waring and Frederick Osius made significant improvements on the original design and began marketing the "Waring Blender." The rest is history.

A blender basically consists of a tall and narrow stainless steel, plastic, or glass food container fitted with metal blades at the bottom. These blades usually have four cutting edges placed on two or four planes allowing for the ingredients in the container to hit multiple cutting surfaces. An upward motion is caused by the rapidly spinning blades, creating a vortex in the container that allows for the incorporation of more air in the final product, giving it a smoother consistency.

When selecting a blender, you should assess certain basic qualities, including its durability, ease of operation and cleaning, capacity, and noise production. With such a wide variety of blenders from which to choose, I hope the following information will help you narrow your choice:

- Blender containers typically come in two sizes: 32 ounces and 40 ounces. If you will routinely be preparing smoothies for more than two people, choose the larger one.

- Blender motors come in different sizes. Those with 290-watt motors are adequate for most blending jobs, but not optimal for smoothies. Others with 330- to 400-watt motors are considered to be of professional caliber and are excellent for crushing ice, a feature that is very important for creating the best smoothies.

- Blenders can be found with a variety of blade speed options, ranging from two speeds (high and low) to multiple (between five and fourteen) speeds. Variable-speed models provide more options, such as the ability to liquefy and whip.

- The blender should have a removable bottom for ease of cleaning.

- Container lids should have a secondary lid that can be easily removed. This allows for the addition of ingredients while the blender is turned on.

- Avoid plastic container jars because they become scratched over time and do not wash well in the dishwasher.

Recently, a new blender that was specifically designed to make smoothies has become available. This whirring wizard, called the Smoothie Elite (by Back to Basics), has several features, including a custom stir stick to break up the air pockets, an ice-crunching blade that assures consistent smoothie texture, and a convenient spigot at the bottom of the container that serves up the finished product.

Although a blender is the ideal appliance for making smoothies, you may prefer a food processor because of its overall versatility or (perhaps more importantly) because it is an appliance you already own. *The New York Times* described the food processor as the "twentieth-century French revolution." This unique appliance can mince, chop, grate, shred, slice, knead, blend, purée, liquefy, and crush ice.

The food processor has a base directly under the work bowl that houses the motor. A metal shaft extending from the base through the center of the work bowl connects the blade or disc to the motor. A cover that fits over the work bowl has a feed tube. When the bowl is locked into place and the motor is switched on, the shaft turns and propels the blades or discs. Unlike the blender container, the food processor bowl is wide and low, causing food to be sent sideways rather than upward by the spinning blade. This motion results in food striking the sides of the container, with less incorporation of air than in the upward motion produced by a blender.

Similar to the blender, the food processor has some basic features you should assess when attempting to select the one that will best fit your cooking needs:

- Food processors come in a wide range of sizes. The 2- or 3-cup mini-processor is practical for chopping, especially small quantities of food. Those with 7-, 9-, and 11-cup capacities are each equally suitable for making smoothies, as well as other food preparations, while 14- and 20-cup units are ideal for professional cooking needs.

- Although a few food processors have four speeds, most have two (high and low), in addition to a pulsing action.

- Some food processors come with both large and small feed tubes. The larger tube is convenient when you're adding large-sized ingredients while the machine is running.

Once you have decided on the features you would like in a blender (or food processor), I encourage you to visit several appliance or department stores and personally view the various models available. The salesclerk should be able to provide you with information to further help you in making the best decision. Another resource for gleaning valuable information is the Internet. Many companies that manufacture these appliances host Web sites that are quite informative about their individual products, and some also provide phone numbers so you can speak personally with representatives. Finally, *Consumer Reports* and similar publications provide comparison ratings concerning the quality of a variety of blenders and food processors.

HELPFUL TECHNIQUES

Now that the blender has taken its rightful place, center stage on your bar or countertop, it is time to rev it up and make a tipsy smoothie. Equipping your kitchen with the necessary tools to make spirited smoothies was relatively easy, and you will be pleased to learn that mastering the techniques required to prepare them is just as simple. In fact, preparing a smoothie may be one of the most uncomplicated tasks you will ever have to perform in your kitchen. Simply place all the appropriate smoothie ingredients in a blender, and you will end up with a very palatable final product.

For those who want to create the ultimate tipsy smoothie, however, here are a few additional techniques that will help you reach that lofty goal:

- To get the most delicious fruit, buy it when it is in season and at its peak in flavor.

- Before freezing fruit, wash and dry it first, then follow the preparation instructions given in chapter 1.

- When you are ready to freeze the fruit, set it in a shallow pan lined with a piece of freezer paper, plastic-coated side facing up, to prevent it from sticking to the surface. In a pinch, you can use parchment or waxed paper. Place the fruit in the freezer for at least 30 minutes or until partially frozen. Using frozen fruit insures that the smoothie will have a thick consistency and also be icy cold.

- Store-bought, individually frozen fruit can be substituted for fresh frozen fruit, but it should be used within six months of the purchase date. Avoid using frozen fruit that is packaged in sweetened syrup.

- To be certain that you have a supply of your favorite seasonal fruits, stock up while they are still available for purchase. Although fruits retain the most flavor when frozen for only one to two weeks, they can be kept in the freezer for eight to twelve months.

- When adding ingredients to a blender, always add the liquid first, then the frozen fruit, and the ice cream or sorbet last. Place all ingredients in a blender, and mix by using the on/off pulse function until the ingredients are mostly blended. Continue mixing, gradually increasing the speed until the mixture is smooth. It takes approximately three to four minutes for a smoothie to reach its optimal consistency. It may be necessary to turn the blender off periodically and stir the mixture with a spoon, working from the bottom up.

- If the fruit you have frozen becomes clumped together, gently pound the fruit pieces within the sealed bag with a mallet or blunt object until they separate.

- If the smoothie is too thin, add more fruit. Conversely, if the smoothie is too thick, add more of your favorite spirit.

GLASSWARE

Choosing an acceptable glass in which to serve a basic smoothie is simply a matter of finding one large enough to hold all the delectable contents. For those who aspire to the next level of tipsy smoothiedom, however, there is an art to choosing the perfect glassware for each specific drink. While a Margarita smoothie may taste delicious served in a tumbler, you can greatly enhance the visual appeal of the drink by offering it in a wide-rimmed Margarita glass, and some say this makes it taste better, too.

Many home bars already have three or four types of specialty glasses, but for those who would like to add a few fun and useful glasses to their existing collection, I will list the types most often suggested for particular drinks found throughout this book. The kind of glasses you choose will depend on which ones best fit your lifestyle and the varieties of tipsy smoothies you prefer, so keep in mind that this list is meant to be informative and not a catalog of glasses that are required:

Champagne
The ideal Champagne glass is either a tall tulip shape or stemmed flute that holds between 6 and 9 ounces.

Wine Glasses/Goblets
Goblets can vary in size and shape, but all have stems and curved sides. They hold from 6 to 20 ounces.

Collins
These stemless glasses are tall and straight-sided and hold from 10 to 14 ounces.

Highball
The Highball glass is similar to a Collins except it is smaller. It holds between 8 and 12 ounces.

Hurricane
A Hurricane is a stemmed glass that resembles a tulip-shaped Champagne glass, except the bowl is wider on the bottom, curves inward midway, and the rim flares out. It holds 15 ounces.

Cocktail/Martini

These long-stemmed glasses have a wide rim and a triangular or V-shaped bowl. They hold between 4 to 12 ounces.

Old-Fashioned

Old-Fashioned glasses are squat, stemless, and have a wide mouth; they hold between 6 and 10 ounces.

Margarita

This glass was designed specifically for the margarita. It is generously sized, stemmed with a wide brim, and holds from 10 to 12 ounces.

Pilsner

A Pilsner is a stemless, tall, narrow glass that holds from 6 to 12 ounces.

Parfait

This is a tall, slender glass with a short stem that holds approximately 7½ ounces.

Whiskey Sour

A Whiskey Sour glass, sometimes called a Delmonico, is a stemmed glass that holds from 4 to 6 ounces.

Cooler

These heavy-duty glasses with a paneled design hold 16 ounces.

Toasting—An Unforgettable Art

✦

*May you live to be 100 years, with
one extra year to repent.*

—A traditional Irish toast

The art of toasting goes back to the sixth century when the Greeks originated the tradition of proposing a drink to the health of their
friends. While this might sound like the polite
thing to do, it was in fact a method of assuring
their guests that the wine wasn't poisoned, a
practice often used in ancient Greece to resolve
social problems. The host would pour wine
from a single pitcher and drink it before his

guests. Once this gesture of good faith satisfied his guests, he would raise his glass and encourage them to do likewise.

The Romans also played a role in the origin of this wonderful tradition. They dropped pieces of burnt bread (toast) into some wines that were not particularly good. This ritual would reduce the acidity of the marginal wine and make it more enjoyable. Hence, the term toasting comes from the Latin word *tostus,* which means parched or roasted.

Finally, a similar tradition can be traced to Olde England, where revelers would commonly place a piece of toast in the bottom of a glass and one would have to drink until he was able to retrieve it.

Today, toasting is a wonderful way of expressing good will toward others, especially when offered on special occasions such as a birthday, wedding, or anniversary celebration. Of course, you don't have to have a reason or an important occasion to share good cheer and health with friends and family. No matter where you are or what the occasion, an engaging toast is always a wonderful prelude to the traditional first sip of a tipsy smoothie. According to Palm Bay Imports (palmbayimports.com), here are a number of traditional toasts from around the world to get you into the spirit. Cheers!

Country	Toast	Pronunciation	Translation
Australia	*Cheers, mate!*	—	—
Canada (English)	*Cheers eh!*	—	—
Canada (French)	*A votre santé!*	*Ah **Vot**-ruh Sahn-**tay***	To your health!
China	*Gan bei!*	*gan-**bay***	Dry your cup!
Croatia	*Zivell!*	***Zhi**-vol-ee*	To life!
Czech Republic	*Na zdravi!*	*Na **zdrah**-vi*	To your health!
Denmark	*Skål!*	—	Cheers!
England	*Cheers!*	—	—
France	*A votre santé!*	*Ah **Vot**-ruh Sahn-**tay***	To your health!
Germany	*Prosit!*	***Proh**-sit*	Cheers!
Greece	*Stin eyiassou!*	*Stin Eye-ee-**yass**-ooh*	To your health!
Hawaii	*Aloha!*	*ä-**lō**-hä*	Hello, goodbye, or love
Hungary	*Lel Lel Lel Egeszsegere!*	*Lay Lay Lay Egg-esh Ay-ged-reh*	Down! Down! Down! Your health!
Ireland	*Sláinte!*	*slahn-cha*	To Your Health!
Israel	*L'Chaim!*	*Le **Hy**-em*	To life!

continued from page 31

Country	Toast	Pronunciation	Translation
Italy	Cin! Cin!	Chin Chin	Cheers!
Jamaica	Cheers, man!	—	—
Japan	Kampai!	Kam-pie	To an empty glass!
Netherlands	Proost!	prohst	Cheers!
Poland	Na zdrowie!	Naz-**dro**-vee-ay	To your health!
Portugal	Saúde!	Sow-**ooh**-jee	Cheers!
Russia	Zdrowie!	Zdo-ro-vee	To your health!
Scotland	Slainte!	slahn-cha	To your health!
Spain	Salud!	Sah-**lud**	To your health!
Sweden	Skål!	Skoll	Cheers!
Turkey	Şerefe!	Share-a-**feh**	To your honor!
United States	Cheers!	—	—
Yiddish	Zei gazunt!	Zye Gah-**zoont**	To your health!

CHAPTER 4

Gin

Martini Smoothies and Beyond

*I exercise strong self-control. I
never drink anything stronger
than gin before breakfast.*

—W. C. FIELDS

Gin is a grain spirit flavored with the aromatic
blue-green berries of the juniper bush.
Along with the berries, each gin maker adds his
or her own assortment of botanicals, or herbs
and spices, to complete a highly guarded secret
formula. These botanicals, which come from all
over the world, include angelica root, cinnamon, anise, coriander, orange peel, and cassia

bark. The number of botanicals gin makers include in their formulas ranges from as few as four or five to as many as fifteen.

Gin was first produced during the Renaissance. In the 1600s, Dr. Franciscus de la Boe (widely known as Dr. Sylvius), a professor of medicine at the University of Leyden in Holland, was seeking ways to treat a variety of tropical diseases suffered by sailors who worked on the Dutch East India Company ships. Because many physicians were having some success using juniper berries to reduce fever, Dr. Sylvius postulated that he could make an infusion of oil out of juniper berries and grain alcohol to treat the maladies of these sailors. Much to his dismay, this infusion did not cure the tropical diseases. However, Dr. Sylvius discovered that it possessed a number of other beneficial qualities, such as acting as a mild diuretic, sedative, appetite stimulant, and a vasodilator that helped a number of heart conditions. Dr. Sylvius called this miracle infusion *aqua vitae,* but his countrymen dubbed it *genever,* which is the Dutch word for juniper.

In addition to Dr. Sylvius's creation of genever, what is even more startling is the fact that he used grain alcohol rather than the more widely used grapes or other fruits to produce a beverage alcohol. Although the Irish and Scotch were using grain to make whiskey, they aged the various grains in wooden casks to refine their taste. Genever was not aged at all, yet it tasted good and at the same time had the benefit of being considerably less expensive to produce.

In the late seventeenth century, English soldiers fighting against the Spanish in the Netherlands during the Thirty Years War, had their first taste of gin and immediately took a liking to it because of its restorative powers and hearty flavor. They called it "Dutch Courage" because it gave them the courage to fight. It wasn't long before seaports became the bustling arenas for this highly popular drink, especially among sailors and soldiers. When the war ended, the soldiers took hefty supplies of genever back to England, where it was already being sold in some chemist shops.

Although distillation of genever was taking place in England at that time, it was on a very small scale. However, when the Dutch Protestant King William III (or William of Orange, as he was better known) and his English wife, Mary, became the co-rulers of England, they wanted to discourage any importation of brandy produced in Catholic wine-making countries. High tariffs were imposed on these brandies, resulting in these French spirits becoming a very costly commodity in the British market. At the same time, he encouraged the production of grain spirits (also known as *corn brandy*) by enacting "An Act for the Encouraging of the Distillation of Brandy and Spirits from Corn." By mass-producing gin, it became an affordable drink that all people could enjoy. Unfortunately, this spirit soon became the favored drink of the poor, resulting in a high rate of alcohol abuse among them. To combat this problem, the Gin Act was issued in 1736, making the production of gin prohibitively expensive. The cost of a license to sell gin retail was increased and the duty was raised on each gallon, with two gallons being the smallest amount one could buy. Predictably, riots broke out and laws were openly broken. Although this Act caused the demise of many legitimate distillers, the production of gin actually rose by almost 50 percent because of the number of illicit distillers.

It soon became very clear that the Gin Act was a failure, so it was repealed in 1742. A new draft was drawn up with the cooperation and input from the distillers, resulting in higher prices, reasonable excise duties, and supervision of licensed distillers. These measures ultimately led to more respectable and higher quality commercial distilling companies.

Several different kinds of gin are currently being produced. The United Kingdom produces mostly *dry* gin (that is, gin that lacks sweetness), or London dry gin, as it is sometimes called. However, this term has now become a generic name to describe a particular style of gin. While the gin is unsweetened, it is accented with the flavor of citrus that comes from the addition of dried lemon and Seville orange peels added to the botanical mixture. Other countries producing dry gin are the United States and Spain.

Dry gin is distilled in continuous column stills, which consist of two enclosed copper or stainless steel columns. Fermented liquid is slowly fed down into the top of the first column while steam is sent up from the bottom. As the steam rises, it strips the alcohol from the descending liquid and carries it over into the second column where it is recirculated and concentrated to the desired percentage of alcohol.

Sloe gin is a sweet, gin-based liqueur flavored with blackthorn, or sloe, plums. It is not a real gin.

Genever is a Dutch style gin produced in the Netherlands. It is made from malted grain mash and distilled in a pot still, which is an enclosed vessel—usually made of copper—into which the liquid mash is placed and heated. The pot has an attached tapered tube at the top to collect alcohol vapor that evaporates when the fermented contents are boiled. The tube bends downward off the top of the pot and runs through a cooling medium, usually a bath of cold water, causing the alcohol vapor to condense back into liquid and drain into a container at the end of the tube.

There are two types of genevers, old *(oude)* and young *(jonge)*, the names referring to the era in which each originated, not the age of the bottled product. *Oude*, the original genever style is straw-colored and relatively sweet and aromatic, while its younger counterpart, *Jonge*, has a drier palate; lighter body; and a smooth, delicate taste. Genever is never used to make a cocktail, but rather it is served chilled and straight up.

Old Tom gin is a lightly sweetened gin that was popular in eighteenth-century England, while Plymouth gin is full-bodied, slightly fruity, and very aromatic. This latter gin is made by one distillery: Croates & Co. in the English Channel port of Plymouth.

Gin's distinctive character and flavor makes it one of the most mixable spirits used to create a cocktail. So, fill a glass full of *Orange Bang! Smoothie*, give an enthusiastic thanks to the wonders of gin, and wish your good friends supreme Dutch happiness by saying *"Proost!"* as you clink their glasses. Cheers!

Barnegat Bay Cooler Smoothie

1 SERVING

¼ cup gin

1 tablespoon club soda

1 teaspoon maraschino liqueur or other cherry
  liqueur

1 teaspoon fresh lime juice

1 teaspoon Sugar Syrup (page 56), or to taste
  (optional)

1½ cups diced pineapple

Place all ingredients in a blender and mix by
using the on/off pulse function until the ingredients are mostly blended. Continue mixing, gradually increasing the speed, until the mixture is
smooth. Pour the smoothie into a glass and garnish with a Pineapple Bow (page 242), if desired.
For an authentic touch, serve the smoothie in an
Old-Fashioned glass.

Bermuda Cocktail Smoothie

1 SERVING

3 tablespoons gin

2 tablespoons apricot brandy

1 teaspoon fresh lime juice

1 teaspoon Sugar Syrup (page 56), or to taste

1 1/2 cups diced apricots

1/2 cup orange sorbet

1/2 teaspoon blue curaçao

Place the gin, apricot brandy, lime juice, Sugar Syrup, apricots, and sorbet in a blender, and mix by using the on/off pulse function until the ingredients are mostly blended. Continue mixing, gradually increasing the speed, until the mixture is smooth. Pour the smoothie into a glass and float blue curaçao on top. Garnish the rim with an Orange Wheel (page 237), if desired. For an authentic touch, serve the smoothie in an Old-Fashioned glass.

Bronx Silver Smoothie

1 SERVING

3 tablespoons gin

1 tablespoon sweet vermouth

1 tablespoon dry vermouth

1 teaspoon Sugar Syrup (page 56), or to taste
  (optional)

1 ½ cups diced orange

½ cup orange sorbet

Place all ingredients in a blender, and mix by
using the on/off pulse function until the ingredients are mostly blended. Continue mixing,
gradually increasing the speed, until the mixture
is smooth. Pour the smoothie into a glass and
garnish the rim with an Orange Wheel (page
237), if desired. For an authentic touch, serve
the smoothie in a Cocktail glass.

Coco Chanel Smoothie

1 SERVING

2 tablespoons gin

2 tablespoons Kahlúa or other coffee liqueur

¾ cup diced banana

¾ cup diced pineapple

1 cup vanilla ice cream

Place all ingredients in a blender, and mix by using the on/off pulse function until the ingredients are mostly blended. Continue mixing, gradually increasing the speed, and blend just until the mixture is smooth. Pour the smoothie into a glass and garnish with a Crisp Banana Wafer (page 235), if desired. For an authentic touch, serve the smoothie in a Cocktail glass.

Cristoforo Columbo Smoothie

1 SERVING

3 tablespoons gin

1 tablespoon Campari

1 ½ cups diced orange

¾ cup orange sorbet

½ teaspoon curaçao

Place the gin, Campari, orange, and sorbet in a blender, and mix by using the on/off pulse function until the ingredients are mostly blended. Continue mixing, gradually increasing the speed, until the mixture is smooth. Pour the smoothie into a glass and float curaçao on top. Garnish the rim of the glass with an Orange Wheel (page 237), if desired. For an authentic touch, serve the smoothie in a Highball glass.

Diamond Head Smoothie

1 SERVING

3 tablespoons gin

1 tablespoon curaçao or other orange liqueur

1 teaspoon sweet vermouth

1 teaspoon Sugar Syrup (page 56), or to taste (optional)

1 ½ cups diced pineapple

Place all ingredients in a blender, and mix by using the on/off pulse function until the ingredients are mostly blended. Continue mixing, gradually increasing the speed, until the mixture is smooth. Pour the smoothie into a glass and garnish with a Pineapple Chip (page 243), if desired. For an authentic touch, serve the smoothie in a Cocktail glass.

Gale Force Smoothie

1 SERVING

3 tablespoons gin

1½ tablespoons plus ½ teaspoon gold rum (page 61)

1 teaspoon Sugar Syrup (page 56), or to taste (optional)

1½ cups diced orange

⅓ cup lemon sorbet

Place the gin, 1½ tablespoons rum, Sugar Syrup, orange, and sorbet in a blender, and mix by using the on/off pulse function until the ingredients are mostly blended. Continue mixing, gradually increasing the speed, until the mixture is smooth. Pour the smoothie into a glass and float the remaining ½ teaspoon rum on top. Garnish with a Fruit Skewer (page 236), if desired. For an authentic touch, serve the smoothie in an Old-Fashioned glass.

Golden Dawn Smoothie

1 SERVING

¼ cup gin

1 ½ tablespoons apricot brandy

1 teaspoon fresh lime juice

1 teaspoon Sugar Syrup (page 56), or to taste
(optional)

Dash of grenadine

1 cup diced apricots

½ cup diced orange

½ cup orange sorbet

Place all ingredients in a blender, and mix by
using the on/off pulse function until the ingredients are mostly blended. Continue mixing,
gradually increasing the speed, until the mixture
is smooth. Pour the smoothie into a glass and
garnish the rim with a Lime Wheel (page 236),
if desired. For an authentic touch, serve the
smoothie in a Cocktail glass.

Great Dane Smoothie

1 SERVING

2 tablespoons gin

1 tablespoon Cherry Heering or other cherry liqueur

1 teaspoon kirsch

1 1/4 cups diced cherries

1 cup vanilla ice cream

Place all ingredients in a blender, and mix by using the on/off pulse function until the ingredients are mostly blended. Continue mixing, gradually increasing the speed, until the mixture is smooth. Pour the smoothie into a glass and garnish with an Almond Pirouette (page 228), if desired. For an authentic touch, serve the smoothie in a Cocktail glass.

Hawaiian Cocktail Smoothie

1 SERVING

$1/4$ cup gin

1 tablespoon triple sec or other orange liqueur

1 $1/2$ cups diced pineapple

$1/2$ cup orange sorbet

Place all ingredients in a blender, and mix by using the on/off pulse function until the ingredients are mostly blended. Continue mixing, gradually increasing the speed, until the mixture is smooth. Pour the smoothie into a glass and garnish the rim with a Pineapple Slice (page 245), if desired. For an authentic touch, serve the smoothie in a Cocktail glass.

Hawaiian Martini Smoothie

1 SERVING

3 tablespoons gin

1/2 teaspoon dry vermouth

1/2 teaspoon sweet vermouth

1 1/2 cups diced pineapple

Place all ingredients in a blender and mix by using the on/off pulse function until the ingredients are mostly blended. Continue mixing, gradually increasing the speed, until the mixture is smooth. Pour the smoothie into a glass and garnish with a Pineapple Bow (page 242), if desired. For an authentic touch, serve the smoothie in a Cocktail glass.

Hawaiian Orange Blossom Smoothie

1 SERVING

3 tablespoons gin

2 tablespoons curaçao or other orange liqueur

1 cup diced orange

½ cup diced pineapple

½ cup orange sorbet

Place all ingredients in a blender, and mix by using the on/off pulse function until the ingredients are mostly blended. Continue mixing, gradually increasing the speed, until the mixture is smooth. Pour the smoothie into a glass and garnish with a Pineapple Chip (page 243), if desired. For an authentic touch, serve the smoothie in a Whiskey Sour glass.

Mandarin Fizz Smoothie

1 SERVING

2 tablespoons gin

2 tablespoons Mandarine Napoleon, Grand
   Marnier, or other orange liqueur

2 tablespoons club soda

1 to 2 teaspoons Sugar Syrup (page 56), or to
   taste (optional)

1 1/2 cups diced orange

1/2 cup orange sorbet

Place all ingredients in a blender, and mix by
using the on/off pulse function until the ingredients are mostly blended. Continue mixing,
gradually increasing the speed, until the mixture
is smooth. Pour the smoothie into a glass and
garnish the rim with an Orange Wheel (page
237), if desired. For an authentic touch, serve
the smoothie in a Highball glass.

Morning Joy Smoothie

1 SERVING

2 tablespoons gin

2 tablespoons crème de banana or other banana
  liqueur

¾ cup diced orange

¾ cup diced banana

½ cup orange sorbet

Place all ingredients in a blender, and mix by
using the on/off pulse function until the ingredients are mostly blended. Continue mixing,
gradually increasing the speed, until the mixture
is smooth. Pour the smoothie into a glass and
garnish with a Crisp Banana Wafer (page 235),
if desired. For an authentic touch, serve the
smoothie in a Whiskey Sour glass.

Orange Bang! Smoothie

1 SERVING

3 tablespoons gin

1 tablespoon triple sec or other orange liqueur

1 ½ cups diced orange

½ cup orange sorbet

Place all ingredients in a blender, and mix by using the on/off pulse function until the ingredients are mostly blended. Continue mixing, gradually increasing the speed, until the mixture is smooth. Pour the smoothie into a glass and garnish the rim with a Lime Wheel (page 237), if desired. For an authentic touch, serve the smoothie in an Old-Fashioned glass.

Polish Sidecar Smoothie

1 SERVING

2 tablespoons gin

2 tablespoons blackberry brandy

1 to 2 teaspoons Sugar Syrup (page 56), or to taste (optional)

1 ¼ cups blackberries

¼ cup lemon sorbet

Place all ingredients in a blender, and mix by using the on/off pulse function until the ingredients are mostly blended. Continue mixing, gradually increasing the speed, until the mixture is smooth. Pour the smoothie into a glass and garnish with Berries on a Skewer (page 232), if desired. For an authentic touch, serve the smoothie in a Cocktail glass.

Royal Orange Blossom Smoothie

1 SERVING

3 tablespoons gin

1 ½ tablespoons Grand Marnier or other
    orange liqueur

1 teaspoon Sugar Syrup (page 56), or to taste

1 ½ cups diced orange

½ cup orange sorbet

Place all ingredients in a blender, and mix by
using the on/off pulse function until the ingredients are mostly blended. Continue mixing,
gradually increasing the speed, until the mixture
is smooth. Pour the smoothie into a glass and
garnish the rim with an Orange, Lemon, and
Cherry Combo (page 239), if desired. For an
authentic touch, serve the smoothie in a Cocktail glass.

Singapore Sling Smoothie

1 SERVING

2 tablespoons gin

1 tablespoon Cherry Heering or other cherry liqueur

1 ½ teaspoons Cointreau, triple sec, or other orange liqueur

1 ½ teaspoons Benedictine

½ teaspoon grenadine

1 ½ cups diced pineapple

¼ cup lemon sorbet

Place all ingredients in a blender, and mix by using the on/off pulse function until the ingredients are mostly blended. Continue mixing, gradually increasing the speed, until the mixture is smooth. Pour the smoothie into a glass and garnish with a Pineapple Bow (page 242), if desired. For an authentic touch, serve the smoothie in a Wine glass.

Sugar Syrup

This isn't a gin recipe, but this syrup is offered as an optional ingredient throughout this book. If you make some and store it, you'll have it on hand, should you choose to include it.

2 CUPS

2 cups granulated (or superfine) sugar

2 cups cold water

Place sugar and water in a medium saucepan over moderate heat an bring to a boil, stirring occasionally to dissolve the sugar. Let simmer for one minute. Allow the syrup to cool. Transfer the syrup to a plastic or glass airtight container and refrigerate. Shake before using.

Tutti-Frutti Smoothie

1 SERVING

3 tablespoons gin

1 ½ tablespoons maraschino liqueur or other cherry liqueur

1 ½ tablespoons Amaretto

1 teaspoon Sugar Syrup (page 56), or to taste (optional)

½ cup diced apple

½ cup diced pear

½ cup diced peach

½ cup peach sorbet

Place all ingredients in a blender, and mix by using the on/off pulse function until the ingredients are mostly blended. Continue mixing, gradually increasing the speed, until the mixture is smooth. Pour the smoothie into a glass and garnish with a Pear Chip (page 240), if desired. For an authentic touch, serve the smoothie in a Highball glass.

Velvet Kiss Smoothie

1 SERVING

2 tablespoons gin

1 tablespoon crème de banana or other banana
   liqueur

Dash of grenadine

1 cup diced pineapple

½ cup diced banana

½ cup vanilla ice cream

Place all ingredients in a blender, and mix by
using the on/off pulse function until the ingredients are mostly blended. Continue mixing,
gradually increasing the speed, until the mixture
is smooth. Pour the smoothie into a glass and
garnish with an Almond Pirouette (page 228),
if desired. For an authentic touch, serve the
smoothie in a Cocktail glass.

CHAPTER 5

Rum*

Smoothies from the Caribbean

You can't lay on the beach and drink rum all day if you don't start in the morning.

—MINISTRY OF RUM
(www.ministryofrum.com)

Although there is much controversy over the origin of the *rum*, it is widely believed that it's a shortened version of the word *Rumbullion*, which is both a Creole word meaning "stem stew" and the English country slang term for "uproar." The first written reference to rum liquor appeared in Barbados in 1651, 25 years after the English settlement of the island.

Rum is distilled from fermented molasses or the juice of the sugarcane. Although most rum is produced in the Caribbean, sugarcane is not native to this region. Spanish explorers brought the plant with them on their journeys to this part of the world. In 1493, Christopher Columbus brought sugarcane cuttings from the Canary Islands and transplanted them on Hispaniola, the Caribbean island that is today shared by the nations of Haiti and the Dominican Republic. This prolific plant not only revolutionized the Caribbean economy, but it had a major impact on the drinking habits of both the Old and New Worlds.

By the seventeenth century, fueled by an ideal climate for growing sugarcane, sugar plantations and mills had become widespread around the Caribbean islands. The mills first crushed the sugarcane to extract its juice, then boiled the juice, which crystallized into chunks of sugar. The remaining unsolidified juice, called molasses, was a sticky syrup with a very high sugar content. Much to their surprise, sugar mill operators soon discovered that when molasses was mixed with water and left out in the sun, it began to ferment. By the 1650s, what was once considered a waste product was suddenly being distilled into spirits that the English colonists dubbed Kill-Devil because it tended to cause nasty hangovers. The locals drank it as a cure-all for many of the maladies that afflicted them, while plantation owners sold the rum at a discount price to naval ships stationed in the Caribbean in hopes of keeping them there to protect the island from pirates. To discourage sailors from getting too drunk while aboard ship, the British Navy issued rations of rum called Grog—a blend of rum, water, and lime juice. This naval connection paved the way for rum's introduction to the outside world, and it soon became a thriving export trade with large amounts being shipped from the Caribbean islands to England, as well as to British colonists living in North America.

The fermentation process that results in rum begins with a small amount of molasses that is first diluted and then mixed with a special yeast. Each strain of yeast is unique to the individual rum distiller, who typically keeps it a closely guarded secret. After seven to ten days, this yeast culture will grow enough to be added to molasses in large fermenting tanks. From this point, the fermentation process takes about 72 hours. Once fermented, the batch is distilled in continuous-column stills. Later, the distilled spirits are aged in oak barrels until mature enough to blend with other rums of various ages and from different batches.

There are many varieties of rum, most of which fall into five categories: white, golden, dark, spice, and añejo.

- *White.* Sometimes designated "silver" or "light," these rums are light-bodied and clear. While most white rums do not age in oak casks, those that do are filtered to remove any color. These rums have a subtle flavor and are used mainly as mixers.

- *Golden or amber.* These contain caramel, which is added for color. These medium-bodied rums age for at least three years in oak barrels and have a smooth, mellow taste.

- *Dark.* These are full-bodied and are more aromatic and richly flavored than their light-bodied cousins. Most are produced from pot stills and then aged in oak barrels from three to twelve years, with caramel being added for color. These delectably rich-flavored rums can be enjoyed straight up.

- *Spice.* Spice is the generic name for any rum that has had a local herb or spice added, infusing it with each island's particular flavor. The most common "spiced" rums are *spice,* enhanced with cinnamon; *nannie,* which has had rosemary added; *l'apsent,* made with absinthe/aniseed; and *pueve,* which is the Creole word for "pepper." These flavorful rums can be white, amber, or dark in color.

- *Añejo. Añejo* is the Spanish word for "aged." These rums are made from different vintages that are carefully blended together to assure that they never vary in flavor from year to year. These golden rums are aged for four to six years in oak barrels, resulting in a rich aroma and a remarkably mellow taste.

Flavored rums such as coconut rums have a natural coconut flavor added. Other rum such as 151 proof, or overproof, rum is usually dark and aromatic, hails from Guyana and the West Indies, and has a higher proof than other rums. 151-proof Demerara rum is made in Guyana and is named after the Demerara River.

The Caribbean ranks as the epicenter of rum production, with each island producing its own signature spirit. Barbados, Cuba, Puerto Rico, Trinidad, and the Virgin Islands are renowned for their light-bodied rums, while the Dominican Republic, Guyana, Haiti, Jamaica, and Martinique are the home of many of the finest full-bodied rums.

Everyone knows that the rich and aromatic flavors of rum marry well with fruit alone, or with a combination of fruit and ice cream. Sounds like a natural ingredient for tipsy smoothies, doesn't it? If you're a Pina Colada lover, I encourage you to transform this Caribbean treat into a smoothie to serve to your friends, then raise your glasses, as the buccaneers did in the seventeenth century—and proclaim, "Yo ho ho and a bottle of fun!"

Apricot Pina Colada Smoothie

1 SERVING

3 tablespoons light rum

1 tablespoon brandy

1 cup diced pineapple

½ cup diced apricots

½ cup coconut gelato or other coconut (or vanilla) ice cream

Place all ingredients in a blender, and mix by using the on/off pulse function until the ingredients are mostly blended. Continue mixing, gradually increasing the speed, until the mixture is smooth. Pour the smoothie into a glass and garnish with a Pineapple Chip (page 243), if desired. For an authentic touch, serve the smoothie in a Collins glass.

Bahama Mama Smoothie

1 SERVING

2 tablespoons light rum

2 tablespoons coconut rum

1 cup diced pineapple

½ cup diced orange

1 tablespoon diced grapefruit

½ cup coconut sorbet

Place all ingredients in a blender, and mix by using the on/off pulse function until the ingredients are mostly blended. Continue mixing, gradually increasing the speed, until the mixture is smooth. Pour the smoothie into a glass and garnish the rim with a Pineapple Wedge (page 245), if desired. For an authentic touch, serve the smoothie in an Old-Fashioned glass.

Blue Hawaiian Smoothie

1 SERVING

2 tablespoons light rum

2 tablespoons blue curaçao

1 ½ cups diced pineapple

½ cup coconut gelato or other coconut (or vanilla) ice cream

Place all ingredients in a blender, and mix by using the on/off pulse function until the ingredients are mostly blended. Continue mixing, gradually increasing the speed, until the mixture is smooth. Pour the smoothie into a glass and garnish the rim with a Pineapple Slice (page 245), if desired. For an authentic touch, serve the smoothie in a Cocktail glass.

Blue Suede Shoes Smoothie

1 SERVING

1 tablespoon coconut rum

1 tablespoon blueberry brandy

1 tablespoon blue curaçao

1 cup diced pineapple

½ cup blueberries

½ cup coconut gelato or other coconut (or vanilla) ice cream

Place all ingredients in a blender, and mix by using the on/off pulse function until the ingredients are mostly blended. Continue mixing, gradually increasing the speed, until the mixture is smooth. Pour the smoothie into a glass and garnish with Berries on a Skewer (page 232), if desired. For an authentic touch, serve the smoothie in a Collins glass.

Bossa Nova

From the Sonesta Beach Hotel, Key Biscayne, Florida

1 SERVING

2 tablespoons light rum

2 tablespoons Galliano

1 1/2 teaspoons apricot brandy

1 cup diced pineapple

1/2 cup diced apricots

1/4 cup lemon sorbet

Place all ingredients in a blender, and mix by using the on/off pulse function until the ingredients are mostly blended. Continue mixing, gradually increasing the speed, until the mixture is smooth. Pour the smoothie into a glass and garnish with a Pineapple Chip (page 243), if desired. For an authentic touch, serve the smoothie in a Pilsner glass.

Caipirissima de Tangerine Smoothie

1 SERVING

¼ cup white rum (or cachaça)*

1 teaspoon Sugar Syrup (page 56), or to taste

1 ½ cups diced tangerines

½ cup orange sorbet

Place all ingredients in a blender, and mix by using the on/off pulse function until the ingredients are mostly blended. Continue mixing, gradually increasing the speed, until the mixture is smooth. Pour the smoothie into a glass and garnish the rim with an Orange Wheel (page 237), if desired. For an authentic touch, serve the smoothie in an Old-Fashioned glass.

*Cachaça is a Brazilian liquor that is directly distilled from the fermented juice of the unrefined sugarcane.

Cantaloupe Cup Smoothie

1 SERVING

3 tablespoons light rum

1 teaspoon fresh lime juice

1 teaspoon Sugar Syrup (page 56), or to taste (optional)

1 cup diced cantaloupe

½ cup diced orange

½ cup orange sorbet

Place all ingredients in a blender, and mix by using the on/off pulse function until the ingredients are mostly blended. Continue mixing, gradually increasing the speed, until the mixture is smooth. Pour the smoothie into a glass and garnish the rim with a Lime Wheel (page 237), if desired. For an authentic touch, serve the smoothie in an Old-Fashioned glass.

Hurricane Smoothie

1 SERVING

2 tablespoons light rum

2 tablespoons dark rum

2 tablespoons 151-proof rum

1 tablespoon grenadine

1 cup diced pineapple

½ cup diced orange

Place all ingredients in a blender, and mix by using the on/off pulse function until the ingredients are mostly blended. Continue mixing, gradually increasing the speed, until the mixture is smooth. Pour the smoothie into a glass and garnish the rim with an Orange Wheel (page 237), if desired. For an authentic touch, serve the smoothie in a Hurricane glass.

Kilauea Lava Flow

From the Hilton Waikoloa Village, Kamuela, Hawaii

1 SERVING

3 tablespoons light rum

1 cup diced pineapple

½ cup strawberries

½ cup coconut gelato or other coconut (or vanilla) ice cream

Place all ingredients in a blender, and mix by using the on/off pulse function until the ingredients are mostly blended. Continue mixing, gradually increasing the speed, until the mixture is smooth. Pour the smoothie into a glass and garnish with a Pineapple Chip (page 243), if desired. For an authentic touch, serve the smoothie in a Hurricane glass.

Mai Tai Smoothie

1 SERVING

2 tablespoons light rum

2 tablespoons curaçao

1 teaspoon fresh lime juice

1 cup diced pineapple

½ cup diced orange

Place all ingredients in a blender, and mix by using the on/off pulse function until the ingredients are mostly blended. Continue mixing, gradually increasing the speed, until the mixture is smooth. Pour the smoothie into a glass and garnish with a fresh orchid, if desired. For an authentic touch, serve the smoothie in an Old-Fashioned glass.

Mango Daiquiri Smoothie

1 SERVING

¼ cup light rum

2 tablespoons curaçao or other orange liqueur

1 teaspoon fresh lime juice

1 teaspoon Sugar Syrup (page 56), or to taste (optional)

1½ cups diced mango

½ cup mango sorbet

Place all ingredients in a blender, and mix by using the on/off pulse function until the ingredients are mostly blended. Continue mixing, gradually increasing the speed, until the mixture is smooth. Pour the smoothie into a glass and garnish the rim with a Lime Wheel (page 237), if desired. For an authentic touch, serve the smoothie in a Wine glass.

Merengue Coffee Smoothie

1 SERVING

2 tablespoons light rum

1 teaspoon Kahlúa or other coffee liqueur

1 teaspoon crème de cacao

¾ cup diced banana

¾ cup diced pineapple

¾ cup coffee ice cream

Place all ingredients in a blender, and mix by using the on/off pulse function until the ingredients are mostly blended. Continue mixing, gradually increasing the speed, just until the mixture is smooth. Pour the smoothie into a glass and garnish with a Cinnamon and Sugar Twist (page 233), if desired. For an authentic touch, serve the smoothie in a coffee mug or Cocktail glass.

Peach Daiquiri Smoothie

1 SERVING

¼ cup light rum

1 teaspoon fresh lime juice

1 teaspoon Sugar Syrup (page 56), or to taste

1½ cups diced peach

½ cup peach sorbet

Place all ingredients in a blender, and mix by using the on/off pulse function until the ingredients are mostly blended. Continue mixing, gradually increasing the speed, until the mixture is smooth. Pour the smoothie into a glass and garnish with a Fruit Skewer (page 236), if desired. For an authentic touch, serve the smoothie in a Wine glass.

Pina Colada Smoothie

1 SERVING

3 tablespoons gold rum

1 tablespoon dark rum

1 1/2 cups diced pineapple

3/4 cup coconut gelato or other coconut (or vanilla) ice cream

Place all ingredients in a blender, and mix by using the on/off pulse function until the ingredients are mostly blended. Continue mixing, gradually increasing the speed, until the mixture is smooth. Pour the smoothie into a glass and garnish with a Pineapple Chip (page 243), if desired. For an authentic touch, serve the smoothie in a Collins glass.

Pink Flamingo Smoothie

1 SERVING

3 tablespoons coconut rum

2 tablespoons Amaretto

1 tablespoon white cranberry juice

1 ½ cups diced pineapple

½ cup coconut gelato or other coconut (or vanilla) ice cream

Place all ingredients in a blender, and mix by using the on/off pulse function until the ingredients are mostly blended. Continue mixing, gradually increasing the speed, until the mixture is smooth. Pour the smoothie into a glass and garnish the rim with an Almond Pirouette (page 228), if desired. For an authentic touch, serve the smoothie in a Hurricane glass.

Raspberry Sparkle Smoothie

1 SERVING

2 tablespoons light rum

2 tablespoons Chambord or other raspberry liqueur

1 teaspoon fresh lime juice

1/2 teaspoon triple sec or other orange liqueur

1 cup diced pineapple

1/2 cup raspberries

1/2 cup orange sorbet

Place all ingredients in a blender, and mix by using the on/off pulse function until the ingredients are mostly blended. Continue mixing, gradually increasing the speed, until the mixture is smooth. Pour the smoothie into a glass and garnish with Berries on a Skewer (page 232), if desired. For an authentic touch, serve the smoothie in a Cocktail glass.

Scorpion Smoothie

1 SERVING

¼ cup light rum

2 tablespoons brandy

1 tablespoon orgeat syrup (a bitter, almond-
flavored syrup) or other almond syrup

1 ½ cups diced orange

¼ cup lemon sorbet

Place all ingredients in a blender, and mix by
using the on/off pulse function until the ingredients are mostly blended. Continue mixing,
gradually increasing the speed, until the mixture
is smooth. Pour the smoothie into a glass and
garnish the rim with an Orange, Lemon, and
Cherry Combo (page 239), if desired. For an
authentic touch, serve the smoothie in a Wine
glass.

Scottish Sunset Smoothie

1 SERVING

2 tablespoons coconut rum

2 tablespoons Scotch

1 tablespoon Grand Marnier or other orange
   liqueur

1 tablespoon grenadine

1 teaspoon Sugar Syrup (page 56), or to taste

1 1/2 cups diced orange

1/2 cup coconut (or orange) sorbet

Place all ingredients in a blender, and mix by
using the on/off pulse function until the ingredients are mostly blended. Continue mixing,
gradually increasing the speed, until the mixture
is smooth. Pour the smoothie into a glass and
garnish the rim with an Orange Wheel (page
237), if desired. For an authentic touch, serve
the smoothie in a Highball glass.

Sex in a Bubblegum Factory Smoothie

1 SERVING

1 tablespoon any rum

1 tablespoon blue curaçao

1 tablespoon crème de banana or other banana liqueur

1 tablespoon lemon-lime soda

¾ cup diced apricots

¾ cup diced banana

Place all ingredients in a blender, and mix by using the on/off pulse function until the ingredients are mostly blended. Continue mixing, gradually increasing the speed, until the mixture is smooth. Pour the smoothie into a glass and garnish with a Crisp Banana Wafer (page 235), if desired. For an authentic touch, serve the smoothie in a Cocktail glass.

Strawberry Banana Colada Smoothie

1 SERVING

2 tablespoons light rum

2 tablespoons dark rum

1 cup diced strawberries

½ cup diced banana

½ cup coconut gelato or other coconut (or vanilla) ice cream

Place all ingredients in a blender, and mix by using the on/off pulse function until the ingredients are mostly blended. Continue mixing, gradually increasing the speed, until the mixture is smooth. Pour the smoothie into a glass and garnish with a Crisp Banana Wafer (page 235), if desired. For an authentic touch, serve the smoothie in a Collins glass.

Strawberry Daiquiri Smoothie

1 SERVING

3 tablespoons light rum

1 teaspoon fresh lime juice

1 teaspoon Sugar Syrup (page 56), or to taste

1 ½ cups diced strawberries

½ cup strawberry sorbet

Place all ingredients in a blender, and mix by using the on/off pulse function until the ingredients are mostly blended. Continue mixing, gradually increasing the speed, until the mixture is smooth. Pour the smoothie into a glass and garnish the rim with a Strawberry Fan (page 247), if desired. For an authentic touch, serve the smoothie in a Cocktail glass.

Strawberry Pina Colada Smoothie #1

1 SERVING

2 tablespoons light rum

2 tablespoons Amaretto

¾ cup diced strawberries

¾ cup diced pineapple

½ cup coconut gelato or other coconut (or vanilla) ice cream

Place all ingredients in a blender, and mix by using the on/off pulse function until the ingredients are mostly blended. Continue mixing, gradually increasing the speed, until the mixture is smooth. Pour the smoothie into a glass and garnish with a Pineapple Chip (page 243), if desired. For an authentic touch, serve the smoothie in a Pilsner glass.

Strawberry Pina Colada Smoothie #2

1 SERVING

¼ cup light rum

1 teaspoon strawberry Schnapps

1 cup diced pineapple

½ cup diced strawberries

½ cup coconut gelato or other coconut (or vanilla) ice cream

Place all ingredients in a blender, and mix by using the on/off pulse function until the ingredients are mostly blended. Continue mixing, gradually increasing the speed, until the mixture is smooth. Pour the smoothie into a glass and garnish with an Almond Pirouette (page 228), if desired. For an authentic touch, serve the smoothie in a Pilsner glass.

The Original Planter's Punch Smoothie

1 SERVING

¼ cup Meyer's dark rum

1 teaspoon fresh lime juice

1 teaspoon superfine (or granulated) sugar

¼ teaspoon grenadine

1 ½ cups diced orange

½ cup orange sorbet

Place all ingredients in a blender, and mix by using the on/off pulse function until the ingredients are mostly blended. Continue mixing, gradually increasing the speed, until the mixture is smooth. Pour the smoothie into a glass and garnish the rim with an Orange, Lemon, and Cherry Combo (page 239), if desired. For an authentic touch, serve the smoothie in a Collins glass.

Waikiki Woo Woo Smoothie

1 SERVING

2 tablespoons any rum

1 tablespoon triple sec or other orange liqueur

1 tablespoon 151-proof rum

1 tablespoon vodka

1 tablespoon tequila

1 tablespoon Amaretto

1 tablespoon white cranberry juice

1 ½ cups diced pineapple

½ cup orange sorbet

Place all ingredients in a blender, and mix by using the on/off pulse function until the ingredients are mostly blended. Continue mixing, gradually increasing the speed, until the mixture is smooth. Pour the smoothie into a glass and garnish the rim with a Pineapple Spear (page 245), if desired. For an authentic touch, serve the smoothie in a Hurricane glass.

Zombie Smoothie

1 SERVING

1 1/2 tablespoons light rum (preferably Puerto Rican)

1 1/2 tablespoons dark rum (preferably Jamaican)

1 tablespoon 151-proof Demerara rum

1 tablespoon curaçao

1 tablespoon orgeat syrup (a bitter, almond-flavored syrup) or Sugar Syrup (page 56), or to taste (optional)

1 teaspoon grenadine

1 cup diced pineapple

1/2 cup diced orange

1/4 cup lemon sorbet

Place all ingredients in a blender, and mix by using the on/off pulse function until the ingredients are mostly blended. Continue mixing, gradually increasing the speed, until the mixture is smooth. Pour the smoothie into a glass and garnish the rim with a Pineapple Wedge (page 245), if desired. For an authentic touch, serve the smoothie in a Collins glass.

CHAPTER 6

Vodka

A Gift from Mother Russia

✦

Call me what you like,
only give me some vodka.

—Russian proverb on name-calling

The word *vodka* comes from the Russian diminutive *voda*, or *little water*. Vodka is made from neutral spirits (distilled spirits made from any material at or above 190 proof, or 95% alcohol). Although vodka was traditionally made from potatoes, premier vodkas of today are made from a variety of cereal grains, including barley, wheat, rye, or corn. Void of any discernable taste, character, color, or odor, vodka's neutral character makes it the quintessential mixer. That's probably why it is among the top-selling spirits in the United States.

Although *vodka* is a Russian word, there has been an ongoing dispute over who invented this spirit, with both Russia and Poland claiming to be its mother country. What we do know for certain is that during the Middle Ages, crude, rye-based vodka was made for medicinal purposes to be used either as an anesthetic or disinfectant. Over time, as people gradually grew accustomed to the spirit and no longer focused on its curative properties, vodka became a popular drink. By the fifteenth century, advances in distilling techniques and surpluses of grain led to the growth of vodka distillation in both Russia and Poland.

The production of vodka starts with the distillation of a fermented mash of grain at a very high (190) proof. This is done to remove any by-products formed during the distillation process that might otherwise lend an unwanted flavor to the spirits. To further purify the resulting product, it is filtered by continuously running it through tanks containing charcoal, resulting in vodka's notably clean taste. In this instance, accolades go to the Russians, specifically Russian chemist Andrey Albanov who invented the filtering technique in 1810. Albanov's process is still being used today.

While the debate continues as to which country deserves credit for inventing vodka, there is no denying that this clean-tasting spirit has enjoyed most favored status in both Russia and Poland for hundreds of years. The citizenry of both nations, who must endure long and harsh winters, discovered that vodka was an effective way to chase the blues. For the same reason, vodka's popularity quickly spread throughout northern Europe, where Scandinavians welcomed the clear liquor for its restorative qualities. However, the Scandinavians flavored their vodka, or *aquavit* ("water of life"), as it is called there, with a variety of herbs and spices, such as dill or caraway.

The story of how Russian vodka found its way to the United States is a long, convoluted tale that has its roots in the Russian Revolution. During this time, the Bolsheviks confiscated all the private distilleries in Moscow, causing a number of Russian vodka makers to emigrate, taking with them their skills and recipes. One appropriated distillery, owned by Piotr Arsenyevitch Smirnov, had the distinction of having been the official purveyor to the Imperial Russian Court since 1886. The owner's son Vladimir, fleeing for his life, went to Turkey, then Poland, and finally ended up in Paris, where he tried to revive his family's business, using the French version of his family name: Smirnoff. Soon thereafter, Vladimir met Rudolf Kunett, a Russian émigré from the United States who was on business in Paris. Mr. Kunett bought the American rights to produce Smirnoff vodka, and the first distillery was set up in the United States in 1934.

Although vodka had been available since the mid-1930s, America's enthusiasm for it did not reach a crescendo until after World War II, when severe shortages of many goods, including liquor, resulted. As the public searched for cocktail ingredients, Smirnoff vodka was found among the scanty bottles of liquor remaining on liquor store shelves. But what really propelled vodka in the limelight was largely a matter of good luck and timing, coupled with a novel idea. Smirnoff had been taken over by the distilling giant, Heublein, Inc.; and in the late 1940s, the president of the company, John Martin, was looking for ways to promote his newly acquired product. While in Hollywood, California, he met Jack Morgan, owner of the Cock 'n' Bull restaurant who was trying to rid himself of an overstock of ginger beer he made on the side. He also had a friend who wanted to dispose of copper mugs made in a copper factory she had inherited. These three individuals came up with a brilliant scheme that would satisfy all of their needs. They concocted a drink called the Moscow Mule—a mixture of Smirnoff vodka, ginger beer, and the juice from half a lime—to be sold in a 5-ounce copper mug embossed with a kicking mule on the side. It became a runaway success and put vodka on the cocktail map in the United States.

With vodka having the highest "mixability" rating of all spirits, it is no wonder that it makes the perfect ingredient to include in a smoothie cocktail. What better way to enjoy this crystal-clear elixir than to fill glasses with a *Black Russian* Smoothie and salute your friends in either Russian *(Zdrowie!)* or Polish *(Na zdrowie!)*. To your health!

'57 T-Bird with Florida Plates Smoothie

1 SERVING

1 tablespoon vodka

1 tablespoon Grand Marnier or other orange liqueur

1 tablespoon Amaretto

1 ½ cups diced orange

½ cup orange sorbet

Place all ingredients in a blender, and mix by using the on/off pulse function until the ingredients are mostly blended. Continue mixing, gradually increasing the speed, until the mixture is smooth. Pour the smoothie into a glass and garnish the rim with a Lime Wheel (page 237), if desired. For an authentic touch, serve the smoothie in a Highball glass.

Alexander Nevsky Cocktail Smoothie

1 SERVING

2 tablespoons vodka

2 tablespoons apricot brandy

1 teaspoon Sugar Syrup (page 56), or to taste
  (optional)

1 cup diced apricots

1/2 cup diced orange

1/4 cup lemon sorbet

Place all ingredients in a blender, and mix by
using the on/off pulse function until the ingredients are mostly blended. Continue mixing,
gradually increasing the speed, until the mixture
is smooth. Pour the smoothie into a glass and
garnish the rim with an Orange Wheel (page
237), if desired. For an authentic touch, serve
the smoothie in a Wine glass.

Banana Split Martini Smoothie

1 SERVING

2 tablespoons vodka

2 tablespoons Godiva White Chocolate Liqueur

1 tablespoon crème de banana or other banana liqueur

1 teaspoon grenadine

1 cup diced banana

1 cup vanilla ice cream

Place all ingredients in a blender, and mix by using the on/off pulse function until the ingredients are mostly blended. Continue mixing, gradually increasing the speed, just until the mixture is smooth. Pour the smoothie into a glass and garnish with an Almond Pirouette (page 228), if desired. For an authentic touch, serve the smoothie in a Cocktail glass.

Black Russian Smoothie

1 SERVING

3 tablespoons vodka

2 tablespoons Kahlúa or other coffee liqueur

¾ cup diced banana

¾ cup diced pineapple

1 cup vanilla ice cream

Place all ingredients in a blender, and mix by using the on/off pulse function until the ingredients are mostly blended. Continue mixing, gradually increasing the speed, just until the mixture is smooth. Pour the smoothie into a glass and garnish with a Cinnamon and Sugar Twist (page 233), if desired. For an authentic touch, serve the smoothie in an Old-Fashioned glass.

Note: To make a White Russian, use the same ingredients in the above recipe except add 3 tablespoons coffee liqueur.

Blue Lagoon Smoothie

1 SERVING

3 tablespoons vodka

1 tablespoon blue curaçao

Several dashes green Chartreuse

1 ½ cups diced pineapple

Place all ingredients in a blender, and mix by using the on/off pulse function until the ingredients are mostly blended. Continue mixing, gradually increasing the speed, until the mixture is smooth. Pour the smoothie into a glass and garnish the rim with a Pineapple Wedge (page 245), if desired. For an authentic touch, serve the smoothie in a Cocktail glass.

Cayman Cup Smoothie

1 SERVING

3 tablespoons vodka

1 tablespoon triple sec or other orange liqueur

1 teaspoon fresh lemon juice

1 ½ cups diced mango

½ cup orange sorbet

Place all ingredients in a blender, and mix by using the on/off pulse function until the ingredients are mostly blended. Continue mixing, gradually increasing the speed, until the mixture is smooth. Pour the smoothie into a glass and garnish with a Fruit Skewer (page 236), if desired. For an authentic touch, serve the smoothie in a Collins glass.

Coffee Cooler Smoothie

1 SERVING

3 tablespoons vodka

2 tablespoons Kahlúa or other coffee liqueur

1 tablespoon crème de banana or other banana liqueur

¾ cup diced banana

¾ cup diced pineapple

1 cup coffee ice cream

Place all ingredients in a blender, and mix by using the on/off pulse function until the ingredients are mostly blended. Continue mixing, gradually increasing the speed, just until the mixture is smooth. Pour the smoothie into a glass and garnish with a Cinnamon and Sugar Twist (page 233), if desired. For an authentic touch, serve the smoothie in an Old-Fashioned glass.

Cosmopolitan Smoothie

1 SERVING

3 tablespoons vodka

2 tablespoons Cointreau, triple sec, or other
   orange liqueur

1 tablespoon white cranberry juice

1 teaspoon fresh lime juice

1 ½ cups diced orange

½ cup orange sorbet

Place all ingredients in a blender, and mix by
using the on/off pulse function until the ingredients are mostly blended. Continue mixing,
gradually increasing the speed, until the mixture
is smooth. Pour the smoothie into a glass and
garnish the rim with a Lime Wheel (page 237),
if desired. For an authentic touch, serve the
smoothie in a Cocktail glass.

Frostini Smoothie

1 SERVING

1 tablespoon vodka

1 tablespoon Godiva White Chocolate Liqueur

1 tablespoon Baileys Original Irish Cream or other Irish cream liqueur

¾ cup diced banana

¾ cup diced pineapple

¾ to 1 cup vanilla ice cream

Place all ingredients in a blender, and mix by using the on/off pulse function until the ingredients are mostly blended. Continue mixing, gradually increasing the speed, until the mixture is smooth. Pour the smoothie into a glass and garnish with an Almond Pirouette (page 228), if desired. For an authentic touch, serve the smoothie in a Cocktail glass.

Fuzzy Navel Smoothie

1 SERVING

2 tablespoons vodka

1 tablespoon peach Schnapps

¾ cup diced orange

¾ cup diced peach

½ cup peach sorbet

Place all ingredients in a blender, and mix by using the on/off pulse function until the ingredients are mostly blended. Continue mixing, gradually increasing the speed, until the mixture is smooth. Pour the smoothie into a glass and garnish the rim with an Orange Wheel (page 237), if desired. For an authentic touch, serve the smoothie in a Collins glass.

Harvey Wallbanger Smoothie

1 SERVING

3 tablespoons vodka

1 1/2 cups diced orange

1/2 cup orange sorbet

1 tablespoon Galliano

Place the vodka, orange, and sorbet in a blender, and mix by using the on/off pulse function until the ingredients are mostly blended. Continue mixing, gradually increasing the speed, until the mixture is smooth. Pour the smoothie into a glass and float Galliano on top. Garnish the rim with an Orange, Lemon, and Cherry Combo (page 239), if desired. For an authentic touch, serve the smoothie in a Collins glass.

Adonis Smoothie

1 SERVING

¼ cup vodka

1 tablespoon apricot brandy

1 teaspoon Sugar Syrup (page 56), or to taste

1 cup diced pineapple

½ cup diced apricots

Place all ingredients in a blender, and mix by using the on/off pulse function until the ingredients are mostly blended. Continue mixing, gradually increasing the speed, until the mixture is smooth. Pour the smoothie into a glass and garnish the rim with a Pineapple Spear (page 245), if desired. For an authentic touch, serve the smoothie in a Cocktail glass.

Mother's Whistler Smoothie

1 SERVING

3 tablespoons vodka

1 tablespoon orgeat syrup (a bitter, almond-
flavored syrup) or other almond syrup

Dash of kirsch

1 ½ cups diced pineapple

Place all ingredients in a blender, and mix by
using the on/off pulse function until the ingredients are mostly blended. Continue mixing, gradually increasing the speed, until the mixture is
smooth. Pour the smoothie into a glass and garnish with a Pineapple Chip (page 243), if desired.
For an authentic touch, serve the smoothie in an
Old-Fashioned glass.

Mystic Cooler Smoothie

From the Royal Sonesta Hotel, New Orleans, Louisiana

1 SERVING

3 tablespoons vodka

1 tablespoon crème de banana or other banana liqueur

1 teaspoon Sugar Syrup or to taste (page 56)

1 cup diced pineapple

½ cup diced banana

2 tablespoons diced red grapefruit or 1 teaspoon grapefruit juice

½ cup orange sorbet

½ to 1 teaspoon grenadine

Place the vodka, banana liqueur, Sugar Syrup, pineapple, banana, grapefruit, and sorbet in a blender, and mix by using the on/off pulse function until the ingredients are mostly blended. Continue mixing, gradually increasing the speed, until the mixture is smooth. Pour the smoothie into a glass and float grenadine on top. Garnish with a Pineapple Bow (page 242), if desired. For an authentic touch, serve the smoothie in a Collins glass.

Orange Delight Smoothie

1 SERVING

2 tablespoons vodka

2 tablespoons curaçao or other orange liqueur

1 teaspoon fresh lime juice

1 ½ cups diced orange

½ cup orange sorbet

Place all ingredients in a blender, and mix by using the on/off pulse function until the ingredients are mostly blended. Continue mixing, gradually increasing the speed, until the mixture is smooth. Pour the smoothie into a glass and garnish the rim with a Lime Wheel (page 237), if desired. For an authentic touch, serve the smoothie in an Old-Fashioned glass.

Peach Tree Street Smoothie

1 SERVING

3 tablespoons vodka

1 ½ tablespoons peach Schnapps

1 tablespoon white cranberry juice

1 cup diced orange

½ cup diced peach

½ cup peach sorbet

Place all ingredients in a blender, and mix by using the on/off pulse function until the ingredients are mostly blended. Continue mixing, gradually increasing the speed, until the mixture is smooth. Pour the smoothie into a glass and garnish with a Pear Chip (page 240), if desired. For an authentic touch, serve the smoothie in a Wine glass.

Peter's Cheer Smoothie

1 SERVING

2 tablespoons vodka

2 tablespoons Cherry Heering or other cherry liqueur

1 tablespoon dry vermouth

1 teaspoon Sugar Syrup (page 56), or to taste (optional)

1 cup diced orange

½ cup diced cherries

½ cup orange sorbet

Place all ingredients in a blender, and mix by using the on/off pulse function until the ingredients are mostly blended. Continue mixing, gradually increasing the speed, until the mixture is smooth. Pour the smoothie into a glass and garnish the rim with an Orange, Lemon, and Cherry Combo (page 239), if desired. For an authentic touch, serve the smoothie in a Cocktail glass.

Puerto Plata Smoothie

1 SERVING

3 tablespoons vodka

1 tablespoon crème de banana or other banana
   liqueur

1 tablespoon orgeat syrup (a bitter, almond-
   flavored syrup) or other almond syrup

1 cup diced pineapple

1/2 cup diced banana

1/4 cup lemon sorbet

Place all ingredients in a blender, and mix by
using the on/off pulse function until the ingredients are mostly blended. Continue mixing, gradually increasing the speed, until the mixture is
smooth. Pour the smoothie into a glass and garnish with a Pineapple Chip (page 243), if desired.
For an authentic touch, serve the smoothie in an
Old-Fashioned glass.

Sex on the Beach Smoothie

1 SERVING

2 tablespoons vodka

2 tablespoons peach Schnapps

1 tablespoon white cranberry juice

1 ½ cups diced pineapple

Place all ingredients in a blender, and mix by using the on/off pulse function until the ingredients are mostly blended. Continue mixing, gradually increasing the speed, until the mixture is smooth. Pour the smoothie into a glass and garnish with a Pineapple Chip (page 243), if desired. For an authentic touch, serve the smoothie in a Highball glass.

Silver Sunset Smoothie

1 SERVING

2 tablespoons vodka

2 tablespoons Campari

1 tablespoon apricot brandy

1 cup diced apricots

1/2 cup diced orange

1/4 cup lemon sorbet

Place all ingredients in a blender, and mix by using the on/off pulse function until the ingredients are mostly blended. Continue mixing, gradually increasing the speed, until the mixture is smooth. Pour the smoothie into a glass and garnish with a Fruit Skewer (page 236), if desired. For an authentic touch, serve the smoothie in a Cocktail glass.

CHAPTER 7

Tequila

Smoothies Go South of the Border

*One tequila, two tequila,
three tequila, floor.*

—GEORGE CARLIN

Tequila is an alcoholic drink that is double distilled from the sap of the sugar-rich heart (pina) of the agave plant. Over 135 species of this plant grace much of the Mexican landscape, and the juices from several of them are fermented and distilled into a variety of alcoholic drinks. Typically, all these drinks are a type of *mezcal,* but not all *mezcals* can be called tequila.

There are five regions in Mexico where tequila can be legally produced. However, the renowned Tequila region, located in the heart of Los Altos de Jalisco, is recognized as having the best conditions for growing the *agave tequilana weber,* or "blue agave," the plant used exclusively in the production of this notable spirit. On the other hand, *mezcal* can be made from several different species of *agave,* including some wild varieties that are grown without pesticides.

The *agave tequilana weber* is often mistaken for a cactus, but this fleshy succulent actually belongs to the lily or amaryllis family. It's easily recognizable because of its long-fibered, lance-shaped leaves that are blue or green in color and coated with a high content of wax that prevents the plant from losing water. Remarkably, archeologists believe this plant has been cultivated for at least 9,000 years.

Tequila has a long and colorful history. Its roots go back to pre-Hispanic times when, according to legend, the indigenous Aztec peoples of Mexico received a message from heaven in the form of a lightning bolt that split open the heart of the agave plant. The heat from the lightning was so intense that it not only burned the heart of the plant, but it fermented the sap. Assuming this was a gift from the gods, the Aztecs drank the sap and called it *pulque.* The natives continued to make this sweet, milky drink by fermenting the sap of an agave. *Pulque* was used for medicinal purposes and, because it was deemed sacred, was consumed at religious ceremonies as well.

When the Spanish conquistadors invaded Mexico in the sixteenth century, they discovered this ancient spirit being produced by the natives. However, with its 30 percent alcohol content, *pulque* wasn't strong enough for their taste, so they "distilled" the fermented juice of an agave in order to make a stronger spirit and, in doing so, created *mezcal*. They continued to experiment by distilling juices from other varieties of agave, until eventually they discovered the blue agave and created the first "tequila wine." The rest is history.

There are fundamentally two basic categories of tequila: 100 percent blue agave tequila and *mixto*. The 100 percent variety is distilled entirely from the fermented juice of blue agave and must be distilled and bottled in Mexico. Tequila that is distilled from as little as 60 percent blue agave juice and combined with sugars, such as sugarcane or brown sugar, is called *mixto*.

Understanding the labeling of tequilas will help you make a good choice on your next trip to the package store. *White* or *silver* (also called *blanco*) tequila is 100 percent blue agave tequila and is not aged. This tequila has the purest bouquet and flavor of agave. *Gold* tequila is a mixto containing additives such as caramel, which is used to add sweetness as well as give it an aged look. These tequilas are mellow and sometimes have a sweet flavor due to the additives.

Reposado ("rested") is 100 percent blue agave tequila that has been stored in oak tanks or barrels for two to twelve months, resulting in a final product that has a mellow taste, pleasing bouquet, and a pale color. Finally, *añejo* is 100 percent blue agave tequila that has been stored in oak for a minimum of one year, resulting in a golden amber color and a smooth, rich, full-bodied taste.

If the conquistadors could only see today how their ambrosial discovery has grown up. Now, with the proper ingredients, any hombre can transform this ancient gift of the gods into a delightful south-of-the-border smoothie masterpiece. One taste and what can you say but . . . *Olé!*

Blue Smoke Smoothie

1 SERVING

3 tablespoons any tequila

1 ½ cups diced orange

½ cup orange sorbet

½ to 1 teaspoon blue curaçao

Place the tequila, orange, and sorbet in a blender, and mix by using the on/off pulse function until the ingredients are mostly blended. Continue mixing, gradually increasing the speed, until the mixture is smooth. Pour the smoothie into a glass and float blue curaçao on top. Garnish the rim with an Orange Wheel (page 237), if desired. For an authentic touch, serve the smoothie in a Wine glass.

Chapultepec Castle Smoothie

1 SERVING

3 tablespoons any tequila

2 tablespoons Grand Marnier or other orange
    liqueur

1 ½ cups diced orange

½ cup orange sorbet

Place all ingredients in a blender, and mix by
using the on/off pulse function until the ingredients are mostly blended. Continue mixing,
gradually increasing the speed, until the mixture
is smooth. Pour the smoothie into a glass and
garnish the rim with an Orange Wheel (page
237), if desired. For an authentic touch, serve
the smoothie in an Old-Fashioned glass.

Coco Loco Smoothie

1 SERVING

2 tablespoons any tequila

2 tablespoons gin

2 tablespoons light rum

1 teaspoon fresh lime juice

1 ½ cups diced pineapple

½ cup coconut gelato or other coconut (or vanilla)
  ice cream

Place all ingredients in a blender, and mix by
using the on/off pulse function until the ingredients are mostly blended. Continue mixing,
gradually increasing the speed, until the mixture
is smooth. Pour the smoothie into a glass and
garnish the rim with a Pineapple Slice (page
245), if desired. For an authentic touch, serve
the smoothie in a hollowed-out coconut shell or
Hurricane glass.

Gringo Swizzle Smoothie

1 SERVING

1/4 cup any tequila

1 tablespoon crème de cassis

1 tablespoon ginger ale

1 teaspoon fresh lime juice

1 cup diced pineapple

1/2 cup diced orange

Place all ingredients in a blender, and mix by using the on/off pulse function until the ingredients are mostly blended. Continue mixing, gradually increasing the speed, until the mixture is smooth. Pour the smoothie into a glass and garnish the rim with an Orange Wheel (page 237), if desired. For an authentic touch, serve the smoothie in a Collins glass.

La Bamba Smoothie

1 SERVING

3 tablespoons gold tequila

1 1/2 tablespoons Cointreau, triple sec, or other orange liqueur

1 cup diced pineapple

1/2 cup diced orange

1/2 cup orange sorbet

1/2 teaspoon grenadine

Place the tequila, orange liqueur, pineapple, orange, and sorbet in a blender, and mix by using the on/off pulse function until the ingredients are mostly blended. Continue mixing, gradually increasing the speed, until the mixture is smooth. Pour the smoothie into a glass and float grenadine on top. Garnish the rim with a Lime Wheel (page 237), if desired. For an authentic touch, rub the rim of a Margarita glass with half of a fresh lime. Dip the rim of the glass in a saucer of granulated sugar, turning the rim in the sugar until it is coated evenly. Pour the smoothie into the glass.

Margarita Smoothie

1 SERVING

3 tablespoons gold tequila

1 tablespoon Grand Marnier or other orange
   liqueur

1 tablespoon Cointreau, triple sec, or other orange
   liqueur

2 tablespoons Sour Mix*

1 teaspoon fresh lime juice

1 1/2 cups diced orange

1/2 cup orange sorbet

Place all ingredients in a blender, and mix by using the on/off pulse function until the ingredients are mostly blended. Continue mixing, gradually increasing the speed, until the mixture is smooth. Pour the smoothie into a glass and garnish the rim with a Lime Wheel (page 237), if desired. For an authentic touch, rub the rim of a Margarita glass with half of a fresh lime. Dip the rim of the glass in a saucer of salt, turning the rim in the salt until it is coated evenly. Pour the smoothie into the glass.

*To make Sour Mix, combine 1/2 cup Sugar Syrup (page 56) and 1/2 cup fresh lemon juice in an airtight container and blend well. Refrigerate and use as needed. Shake before using.

Mexican Tangerine Smoothie

1 SERVING

3 tablespoons gold tequila

2 tablespoons Mandarine Napolean, Grand Marnier, or other orange liqueur

1 ½ teaspoons grenadine

1 teaspoon fresh lime juice

1 ½ cups diced tangerines

½ cup orange sorbet

Place all ingredients in a blender, and mix by using the on/off pulse function until the ingredients are mostly blended. Continue mixing, gradually increasing the speed, until the mixture is smooth. Pour the smoothie into a glass and garnish the rim with an Orange Wheel (page 237), if desired. For an authentic touch, serve the smoothie in a Cocktail glass.

Peachtree Margarita Smoothie

1 SERVING

3 tablespoons any tequila

2 tablespoons peach Schnapps

1 teaspoon fresh lime juice

1 1/2 cups diced peach

1/2 cup peach sorbet

Place all ingredients in a blender, and mix by using the on/off pulse function until the ingredients are mostly blended. Continue mixing, gradually increasing the speed, until the mixture is smooth. Pour the smoothie into a glass and garnish the rim with an Orange Wheel (page 237), if desired. For an authentic touch, serve the smoothie in a Margarita glass.

Pina Smoothie

1 SERVING

3 tablespoons any tequila

1 teaspoon Sugar Syrup (page 56), or to taste

1 teaspoon fresh lime juice

1 ½ cups diced pineapple

Place all ingredients in a blender, and mix by using the on/off pulse function until the ingredients are mostly blended. Continue mixing, gradually increasing the speed, until the mixture is smooth. Pour the smoothie into a glass and garnish the rim with a Lime Wheel (page 237), if desired. For an authentic touch, serve the smoothie in an Old-Fashioned glass.

Pineapple Margarita Smoothie

1 SERVING

2 tablespoons any tequila

1 tablespoon triple sec or other orange liqueur

1 teaspoon fresh lime juice

1 ½ cups diced pineapple

Place all ingredients in a blender, and mix by using the on/off pulse function until the ingredients are mostly blended. Continue mixing, gradually increasing the speed, until the mixture is smooth. Pour the smoothie into a glass and garnish the rim with a Pineapple Spear (page 245), if desired. For an authentic touch, serve the smoothie in a Margarita glass.

Royal Matador Smoothie

1 SERVING

3 tablespoons gold tequila

1 ½ tablespoons framboise or other raspberry
   liqueur

1 teaspoon fresh lime juice

½ teaspoon orgeat syrup (a bitter, almond-
   flavored syrup) or other almond syrup

1 ½ cups diced pineapple

½ cup diced banana

½ cup orange sorbet

Place all ingredients in a blender, and mix by
using the on/off pulse function until the ingredients are mostly blended. Continue mixing,
gradually increasing the speed, until the mixture
is smooth. Pour the smoothie into a glass and
garnish with Berries on a Skewer (page 232), if
desired. For an authentic touch, serve the
smoothie in a hollowed-out pineapple shell.

Sauzaliky Smoothie

1 SERVING

3 tablespoons any tequila

1 teaspoon fresh lime juice

1 cup diced orange

½ cup diced banana

½ cup orange sorbet

Place all ingredients in a blender, and mix by using the on/off pulse function until the ingredients are mostly blended. Continue mixing, gradually increasing the speed, until the mixture is smooth. Pour the smoothie into a glass and garnish the rim with an Orange Wheel (page 237), if desired. For an authentic touch, serve the smoothie in a hollowed-out pineapple shell or Wine glass.

Strawberry Margarita Smoothie

1 SERVING

3 tablespoons white tequila

1 tablespoon triple sec or other orange liqueur

1 tablespoon strawberry Schnapps

1 teaspoon fresh lime juice

1 teaspoon Sugar Syrup (page 56), or to taste

1 ½ cups diced strawberries

½ cup strawberry sorbet

Place all ingredients in a blender, and mix by using the on/off pulse function until the ingredients are mostly blended. Continue mixing, gradually increasing the speed, until the mixture is smooth. Pour the smoothie into a glass and garnish the rim with a Strawberry Fan (page 247), if desired. For an authentic touch, serve the smoothie in a Margarita glass.

Tequila Comfort Smoothie

1 SERVING

1 ½ tablespoons gold tequila

2 tablespoons Southern Comfort

1 ½ cups diced orange

½ cup orange sorbet

½ teaspoon raspberry syrup (optional)

Place the tequila, Southern Comfort, orange, and sorbet in a blender, and mix by using the on/off pulse function until the ingredients are mostly blended. Continue mixing, gradually increasing the speed, until the mixture is smooth. Pour the smoothie into a glass and float optional raspberry syrup on top. Garnish with Berries on a Skewer (page 232), if desired. For an authentic touch, serve the smoothie in a Whiskey Sour glass.

Tequila Sunrise Smoothie

1 SERVING

3 tablespoons any tequila

1 teaspoon fresh lime juice

1 ½ cups diced orange

½ cup orange sorbet

1 teaspoon grenadine

Place the tequila, lime juice, orange, and sorbet in a blender, and mix by using the on/off pulse function until the ingredients are mostly blended. Continue mixing, gradually increasing the speed, until the mixture is smooth. Pour the smoothie into a glass and float grenadine on top. Garnish the rim with a Lime Wheel (page 237), if desired. For an authentic touch, serve the smoothie in a Collins glass.

Tequila Sunset Smoothie

1 SERVING

2 tablespoons any tequila

1 ½ cups diced orange

½ cup orange sorbet

1 tablespoon blackberry brandy

Place the tequila, orange, and sorbet in a blender, and mix by using the on/off pulse function until the ingredients are mostly blended. Continue mixing, gradually increasing the speed, until the mixture is smooth. Pour the smoothie into a glass and float blackberry brandy on top. Garnish the rim with an Orange Wheel (page 237), if desired. For an authentic touch, serve the smoothie in a Collins glass.

Tres Compadres Margarita Smoothie

1 SERVING

2 tablespoons gold tequila (preferably Sauza Conmemorativo Añejo)

2 tablespoons Sour Mix (page 123)

1 tablespoon Cointreau, triple sec, or other orange liqueur

1 tablespoon Chambord or other raspberry liqueur

1 teaspoon fresh lime juice

1½ cups diced orange

½ cup orange sorbet

1 teaspoon grenadine

Place the tequila, Sour Mix, orange liqueur, raspberry liqueur, lime juice, orange, and sorbet in a blender, and mix by using the on/off pulse function until the ingredients are mostly blended. Continue mixing, gradually increasing the speed, until the mixture is smooth. Pour the smoothie into a glass and float grenadine on top. Garnish the rim with a Lime Wheel (page 237), if desired. For an authentic touch, rub the rim of a Margarita glass with half of a fresh lime. Dip the rim of the glass in a saucer of salt, turning the rim in the salt until it is coated evenly. Pour the smoothie into the glass.

CHAPTER 8

Whiskey (or Whisky)

Smoothies Meet Jack Daniels

Always carry a large flagon
of whiskey in case of snakebite
and furthermore
always carry a snake.

—W. C. FIELDS

Whiskey (or whisky) is a liquor that is distilled from corn or grains such as barley, rye, or wheat. To immediately clear up the confusion over the spelling of the word, the Irish and Americans spell whiskey with an "e," while the Canadians and Scotch spell it without the "e." All whiskeys begin with a mash (a mixture of crushed grain and hot water) that is fermented by the addition of yeast. There are four basic categories of whiskey: Irish, Scotch, American, and Canadian.

IRISH WHISKEY

It is widely accepted that whiskey originated in Ireland. While the art of distillation had been around for thousands of years, it's believed that in the sixth century Irish monks traveling to the Middle East observed how an *alembic* (a type of pot still) could be used to distill perfume. Upon returning to the Emerald Isle, the monks invented their own pot still to be used for a totally different purpose. They discovered that when they fermented a mash of barley and water with yeast and then heated it in an alembic, the alcohol from the mixture could be separated and retained. The Celtic population called these newly discovered spirits *Uisce Beatha,* "The Water of Life."

Fifteen hundred years later, Irish whiskey is still being made from barley and water. Today, some of the barley is first malted, which means it's allowed to sprout, and then at just the right time, the growing process is halted by drying it in smokeless kilns. The barley is then ground together with rye, corn, and cereal grains before being mixed with water and triple-distilled in copper pot stills. The precious liquid that results from this process is then aged from three to nine years in brandy, sherry, port, bourbon, or rum oak casks, yielding a full-bodied product with a smooth, malty flavor that would put a smile on any leprechaun's face.

SCOTCH WHISKY

The earliest historical reference to the distillation of whisky in Scotland is in a document found in the Scottish Exchequer Rolls of the year 1494, wherein it is stated: "Eight bolls of malt to Friar John Cor wherewith to make aqua vitae." Although highlanders are believed to have been operating stills for several hundred years before that, it was those industrious Irish monks who are credited with the fifteenth-century introduction of the spirits we know today as Scotch whisky.

Beginning in the nineteenth century—and continuing today—large quantities of whisky made from grains other than barley were produced, thanks to Aeneas Coffey, who invented the "continuous still," also known as the "Patent" or "Coffey" still. This innovation allowed for uninterrupted distillation and was soon followed by the advent of blended Scotch whisky, made from a mixture of as many as 50 individual Scotch malt and Scotch grain whiskies from various distillers. Each blending company keeps its unique formula for the proportions a well-guarded secret, and its finished product an unvarying blend that remains recognizable to every customer. Because blends are made by combining whiskies of all ages, the law requires that the age on the label refer to the youngest one used.

There are two varieties of Scotch whisky: malt and grain. Malt whisky is made exclusively from a mixture of specially selected barley, water, and yeast that is distilled in a copper pot still, whereas grain whisky is made from a mixture of unmalted barley, rye, corn, and wheat and is distilled in the Patent, or Coffey, still.

Today, one of the most expensive categories of Scotch whisky, highly favored by connoisseurs, is the single malt variety. To qualify for this prestigious designation, a whisky must meet three requirements:

1. It must be made from malted barley. Unlike Irish whiskey, the sprouted barley used for the Scotch variety is dried in kilns fired by peat, which imparts a highly distinctive smoky character to the finished alcoholic product.

2. A single malt Scotch whisky must be produced by one distillery.

3. After distillation, it must be aged in wooden barrels for a minimum of three years, with the entire process taking place within Scotland. There are over 100 malt whisky distilleries found throughout Scotland, and each produces a single-malt whisky with its own distinctive flavor.

In contrast to single malt whiskies, the vatted malt variety contains a number of malt whiskies that have been carefully blended together to create a consistent whisky, each with its own distinct, identifiable character. This product can consist entirely of single malt whiskies of various ages from the same distillery, or the single malt products of a variety of distilleries.

AMERICAN WHISKEY

Bourbon whiskeys are widely recognized as America's native spirit. While all bourbons are whiskey, not all whiskeys are bourbon. According to United States federal law, bourbon whiskey must be made from mash grain that contains between 51 percent and 79 percent of corn, the remaining grain components being rye or barley. Moreover, blending is not allowed, and additives are forbidden other than water to reduce the proof. Finally, bourbon must be distilled to between 80 to 160 proof and aged at least two years in new, charred oak casks.

The bottle label found on many fine bourbons contains the phrase "sour mash." This refers to the yeasting process whereby liquid is drained from a mash of fermented, cooked grains from a previous distillation, and a certain proportion of this spent mash is added to a fresh mash of cooked grains and yeast, which is then fermented for the new batch.

Although bourbon whiskey can be distilled anywhere in the United States, most is produced in the state of Kentucky, where it must be distilled and warehoused for at least a year in order to be labeled "Kentucky Bourbon." Because bourbon is made with corn, it is a little sweeter and heavier in texture than other whiskeys.

Not to be outdone by Kentucky, neighboring Tennessee also boasts a whiskey made within its borders. Tennessee whiskey, which is very much like bourbon, has a grain content that must be at least 51 percent corn, the remainder consisting of any other grain, such as barley and rye. Its production is similar to the way sour mash bourbon is made, but Tennessee whiskey goes through an additional step, which includes filtering the distilled spirits through thick beds of sugar-maple charcoal in large wooden vats before aging in order to remove any impurities. This final step results in a whiskey that has a smooth and mellow taste.

American blended whiskey is another category of domestically produced whiskey. It dates back to the nineteenth century when continuous stills were invented, allowing for the distillation of neutral spirits (distilled spirits made from any material at or above 190 proof). These whiskeys are made by carefully blending straight whiskey with neutral spirits in varying proportions.

CANADIAN WHISKY

Canadian whisky is a grain product distilled mostly from corn, along with small quantities of rye, wheat, and barley. Although Canadian whisky is often thought of as straight rye whisky, this grain is not the predominant ingredient, although its spicy and bitter-sweet characteristics contribute the most flavor to the blends. Canada does not mandate a specific grain mixture, proof level, or type of storage barrel for the whisky bearing its name. Instead, each individual distiller makes those decisions. On the other hand, U.S. regulations require that any spirits bearing the name Canadian whisky must be legally produced in Canada, aged in charred oak barrels for a minimum of three years (although most age for six to eight years), and be a blend.

Once the whisky has aged, it is carefully combined with mature whiskies of different ages and character in order to produce a consistent blend from year to year. Some of the larger producers have several distilleries in Canada that may use many different yeasts, resulting in more than 50 different straight whiskies that are available for blending. As a rule, Canadian practice is to use about 20 different whiskies in a single blended product. Each distiller's formula calls for varying amounts of the individual grains, with the exact proportions kept confidential. Like other whiskies, the bottle label can only carry the age statement of the youngest whisky used. Canadian whiskies are light-bodied, slightly pale, and mellow.

As you can see, whiskey has a fascinating history, and there are enough varieties to satisfy many different tastes. As for your personal preference, whether you like your whiskey straight or blended, and whether you spell it with or without an "e," you'll be impressed with the flavorful result when your favorite amber ambrosia is included in a refreshing smoothie. So get into the "spirit" by inviting some friends over to your private pub to enjoy a Parknasilla Peg Leg Smoothie and saluting them with a Gaelic toast . . . *Sláinte!* To your health!

Aberdeen Sour Smoothie

1 SERVING

1/4 cup Scotch

1 tablespoon triple sec or other orange liqueur

2 teaspoons fresh lemon juice

1 1/2 cups diced orange

1/2 cup orange sorbet

Place all ingredients in a blender, and mix by using the on/off pulse function until the ingredients are mostly blended. Continue mixing, gradually increasing the speed, until the mixture is smooth. Pour the smoothie into a glass and garnish the rim with an Orange, Lemon, and Cherry Combo (page 239), if desired. For an authentic touch, serve the smoothie in an Old-Fashioned glass.

Algonquin Smoothie

1 SERVING

3 tablespoons blended whiskey

2 tablespoons dry vermouth

1 teaspoon Sugar Syrup (page 56), or to taste (optional)

1 ½ cups diced pineapple

Place all ingredients in a blender, and mix by using the on/off pulse function until the ingredients are mostly blended. Continue mixing, gradually increasing the speed, until the mixture is smooth. Pour the smoothie into a glass and garnish with a Pineapple Chip (page 243), if desired. For an authentic touch, serve the smoothie in a Cocktail glass.

Anchors Aweigh Smoothie

1 SERVING

2 tablespoons bourbon

2 teaspoons triple sec or other orange liqueur

2 teaspoons peach brandy

2 teaspoons maraschino liqueur or other cherry liqueur

1/4 teaspoon maraschino juice

1 cup diced peach

1/2 cup diced orange

1/2 cup vanilla ice cream

Place all ingredients in a blender, and mix by using the on/off pulse function until the ingredients are mostly blended. Continue mixing, gradually increasing the speed, until the mixture is smooth. Pour the smoothie into a glass and garnish with a maraschino cherry, if desired. For an authentic touch, serve the smoothie in an Old-Fashioned glass.

Bandana Smoothie

1 SERVING

3 tablespoons blended whiskey

1 ½ tablespoons crème de banana or other banana liqueur

1 cup diced banana

½ cup diced orange

½ cup orange sorbet

Place all ingredients in a blender, and mix by using the on/off pulse function until the ingredients are mostly blended. Continue mixing, gradually increasing the speed, until the mixture is smooth. Pour the smoothie into a glass and garnish with a Crisp Banana Wafer (page 235), if desired. For an authentic touch, serve the smoothie in a Cocktail glass.

Canadian Stone Fence Smoothie

1 SERVING

3 tablespoons Canadian whisky

1 tablespoon triple sec or other orange liqueur

1 teaspoon Sugar Syrup (page 56), or to taste

1 ½ cups diced apple

½ cup orange sorbet

Place all ingredients in a blender, and mix by using the on/off pulse function until the ingredients are mostly blended. Continue mixing, gradually increasing the speed, until the mixture is smooth. Pour the smoothie into a glass and garnish with an Apple Chip (page 230), if desired. For an authentic touch, serve the smoothie in a Cocktail glass.

Hawaiian Eye Smoothie

1 SERVING

3 tablespoons bourbon

2 tablespoons Kahlúa or other coffee liqueur

1 tablespoon crème de banana or other banana
    liqueur

1 cup diced pineapple

½ cup diced banana

½ cup vanilla ice cream

Place all ingredients in a blender, and mix by
using the on/off pulse function until the ingredients are mostly blended. Continue mixing,
gradually increasing the speed, until the mixture is smooth. Pour the smoothie into a glass
and garnish with a Pineapple Bow (page 242),
if desired. For an authentic touch, serve the
smoothie in a Highball glass.

Indian River Cocktail Smoothie

1 SERVING

2 tablespoons rye (or blended) whiskey

2 tablespoons dry vermouth

1 teaspoon Sugar Syrup (page 56), or to taste
   (optional)

1 1/2 cups diced orange

1/2 cup orange sorbet

Several dashes raspberry syrup

Place the whiskey, vermouth, Sugar Syrup, orange, and sorbet in a blender, and mix by using
the on/off pulse function until the ingredients
are mostly blended. Continue mixing, gradually
increasing the speed, until the mixture is
smooth. Pour the smoothie into a glass and
float raspberry syrup on top. Garnish with
Berries on a Skewer (page 232), if desired. For
an authentic touch, serve the smoothie in an
Old-Fashioned glass.

Kentucky Orange Blossom Smoothie

1 SERVING

3 tablespoons bourbon

1 tablespoon triple sec or other orange liqueur

1 ½ cups diced orange

½ cup orange sorbet

Place all ingredients in a blender, and mix by using the on/off pulse function until the ingredients are mostly blended. Continue mixing, gradually increasing the speed, until the mixture is smooth. Pour the smoothie into a glass and garnish the rim with an Orange, Lemon, and Cherry Combo (page 239), if desired. For an authentic touch, serve the smoothie in an Old-Fashioned glass.

Parknasilla Peg Leg Smoothie

1 SERVING

3 tablespoons Irish whiskey

1 tablespoon club soda

1 teaspoon fresh lemon juice

1 ½ cups diced pineapple

½ cup coconut gelato or other coconut (or vanilla) ice cream

Place all ingredients in a blender, and mix by using the on/off pulse function until the ingredients are mostly blended. Continue mixing, gradually increasing the speed, until the mixture is smooth. Pour the smoothie into a glass and garnish with a Pineapple Chip (page 243), if desired. For an authentic touch, serve the smoothie in a Highball glass.

Red Hot Lovin' Smoothie

1 SERVING

1 tablespoon bourbon

1 tablespoon Amaretto

1 tablespoon Southern Comfort

1 teaspoon sloe gin

½ teaspoon triple sec or other orange liqueur

1 ½ cups diced pineapple

½ cup orange sorbet

Place all ingredients in a blender, and mix by using the on/off pulse function until the ingredients are mostly blended. Continue mixing, gradually increasing the speed, until the mixture is smooth. Pour the smoothie into a glass and garnish with a Pineapple Spear (page 245), if desired. For an authentic touch, serve the smoothie in a Hurricane glass.

Scottish Cobbler Smoothie

1 SERVING

3 tablespoons Scotch

1 tablespoon curaçao or other orange liqueur

1 ½ cups diced pineapple

Place all ingredients in a blender, and mix by using the on/off pulse function until the ingredients are mostly blended. Continue mixing, gradually increasing the speed, until the mixture is smooth. Pour the smoothie into a glass and garnish with Mint Leaves (page 238), if desired. For an authentic touch, serve the smoothie in an Old-Fashioned glass.

Shamrock Smoothie

1 SERVING

3 tablespoons Irish whiskey

3 tablespoons green crème de menthe

¾ cup diced banana

¾ cup diced pineapple

½ to ¾ cup vanilla ice cream

Place all ingredients in a blender, and mix by using the on/off pulse function until the ingredients are mostly blended. Continue mixing, gradually increasing the speed, just until the mixture is smooth. Pour the smoothie into a glass and garnish with a Crisp Banana Wafer (page 235), if desired. For an authentic touch, serve the smoothie in a Wine glass.

Southern Fizz Smoothie

1 SERVING

3 tablespoons blended whiskey (or bourbon)

1 tablespoon Southern Comfort

1 teaspoon orgeat syrup (a bitter, almond-flavored syrup) or other almond syrup

1 teaspoon fresh lemon juice (optional)

1 ½ cups diced orange

½ cup orange sorbet

Place all ingredients in a blender, and mix by using the on/off pulse function until the ingredients are mostly blended. Continue mixing, gradually increasing the speed, until the mixture is smooth. Pour the smoothie into a glass and garnish the rim with an Orange Wheel (page 237), if desired. For an authentic touch, serve the smoothie in a Collins glass.

T-Bird Smoothie

1 SERVING

3 tablespoons Canadian whisky

2 tablespoons Amaretto

1 teaspoon Sugar Syrup (page 56), or to taste

½ teaspoon grenadine

1 cup diced pineapple

½ cup diced orange

Place all ingredients in a blender, and mix by using the on/off pulse function until the ingredients are mostly blended. Continue mixing, gradually increasing the speed, until the mixture is smooth. Pour the smoothie into a glass and garnish the rim with an Orange, Lemon, and Cherry Combo (page 239), if desired. For an authentic touch, serve the smoothie in a Highball glass.

Wicklow Cooler Smoothie

1 SERVING

3 tablespoons Irish whiskey

2 tablespoons dark rum

½ tablespoon ginger ale

1 teaspoon fresh lime juice

1 teaspoon Sugar Syrup (page 56), or to taste

1 ½ cups diced orange

½ cup orange sorbet

Place all ingredients in a blender, and mix by using the on/off pulse function until the ingredients are mostly blended. Continue mixing, gradually increasing the speed, until the mixture is smooth. Pour the smoothie into a glass and garnish with a maraschino cherry, if desired. For an authentic touch, serve the smoothie in a Collins glass.

CHAPTER 9

Liqueur

Elegance in a Smoothie Glass

I feel the end approaching.
Quick, bring me my dessert,
coffee, and liqueur.

—BRILLAT-SAVARIN'S
GREAT-AUNT PIERETTE

Liqueurs (or *cordials* as they are sometimes called) are sweet, highly refined, spirit-based drinks—infused with a variety of natural flavors such as fruit, herb mixtures, or spices and enhanced with sweeteners.

The origin of liqueurs has its roots in the ancient traditions of using certain herbs, seeds, bark, spices, flowers, and fruit as drugs and medicines to relieve a variety of ailments. By the fourth century, alchemists had discovered that the medicinal value of these materials could be preserved for a longer period of time if they were infused with alcohol. In addition, the monks of this era prepared liqueurs from these same components in hopes of finding the "elixir" of eternal youth.

The earliest writings concerning flavored alcohol are those of Arnold de Vila Nova, an alchemist born in 1240 who practiced his art in Spain and France. He described distilling wine into *aqua vitae* and then flavoring it with a variety of herbs and spices. He also wrote widely of the restorative and life-giving attributes of liqueurs. Because of these impressive-sounding properties, many believed that the production of these spirits was a divinely inspired gift from Heaven.

These "waters," or early liqueurs, were first used only as tonics, aphrodisiacs, love potions, or disease preventatives. They eventually became popular as a pleasurable drink, at first in Italy in the fourteenth century, and then in France 200 years later when Catherine de Medici, a native of Tuscany, married Henry II of France in 1533. Not only did the Queen introduce the fashion of drinking liqueur to the French court, but she was also skilled in the art of distillation. By creating her own liqueurs and sharing them with her royal associates, these spirits quickly became a very popular indulgence among the nobility of France.

Between the fourteenth and early seventeenth centuries, most liqueurs were produced by alchemists and the monastic orders. The renowned liqueur Benedictine, for example, was developed in the Abbey of Fecamp in Italy by the Benedictine monk Dom Bernardo Vincelli in the year 1510. By the end of the sixteenth century, however, the production of liqueurs was no longer the sole province of the clergy, and several distilleries had been formed to produce commercial quantities of these flavorful spirits.

Liqueur comes from the Latin word, *liquefacere,* which means to melt or to dissolve. It also refers to the way liqueur is produced. Brandy, whiskey, or other distilled spirits form the base of a liqueur, into which flavor derived from fruit, bark, flowers, herbs and spices, vanilla and coffee beans, or nuts is dissolved. This is accomplished by one of several methods, depending on the source or the particular flavor desired. No matter which production technique is used, however, all liqueurs must be sweetened and contain at least 2.5 percent sugar by weight.

There are different types and brands of liqueurs, and they are divided into two distinct classes: generic products and proprietary brands. The generic liqueurs are produced by a number of manufacturers and are known by their trade name. They encompass all the basic flavors from whatever flavoring agent is used by the individual distiller—such as crème de cacao, crème de menthe, or peach-flavored brandy. Proprietary brands—such as Grand Marnier,

Benedictine, and Cointreau—are generally produced by a single distiller who has the exclusive rights to produce and sell its own product, often using a centuries-old secret formula known to only a very select circle of people.

The inherent sweetness of liqueurs makes them a perfect start for creating an impressive smoothie. So, whether you're married to a French king or just looking for a royal treat after work, try a liqueur-infused smoothie and raise your glass to the sound of *Cin Cin!*

Abbot's Delight Smoothie

1 SERVING

3 tablespoons Frangelico or other hazelnut liqueur

1 cup diced pineapple

½ cup diced banana

Place all ingredients in a blender, and mix by using the on/off pulse function until the ingredients are mostly blended. Continue mixing, gradually increasing the speed, until the mixture is smooth. Pour the smoothie into a glass and garnish with a Pineapple Chip (page 243), if desired. For an authentic touch, serve the smoothie in a Parfait glass.

Acapulco Joy Smoothie

1 SERVING

3 tablespoons Kahlúa or other coffee liqueur

2 tablespoons peach brandy

1 cup diced peach

½ cup diced banana

½ cup vanilla ice cream

Place all ingredients in a blender, and mix by using the on/off pulse function until the ingredients are mostly blended. Continue mixing, gradually increasing the speed, until the mixture is smooth. Pour the smoothie into a glass and garnish with nutmeg and a maraschino cherry, if desired. For an authentic touch, serve the smoothie in a Wine glass.

Banshee Berry Smoothie

1 SERVING

1 ½ tablespoons *crème de banana* or other
banana liqueur

1 ½ tablespoons strawberry *Schnapps*

1 ½ tablespoons *crème de cacao*

¾ cup diced banana

¾ cup diced strawberries

½ cup vanilla ice cream

Place all ingredients in a blender, and mix by using the on/off pulse function until the ingredients are mostly blended. Continue mixing, gradually increasing the speed, just until the mixture is smooth. Pour the smoothie into a glass and garnish with a Strawberry Fan (page 247), if desired. For an authentic touch, serve the smoothie in a Cocktail glass.

Birky's Bubblegum Smoothie

1 SERVING

1 ½ tablespoons blue curaçao

1 ½ tablespoons crème de banana or other
banana liqueur

1 tablespoon Baileys Original Irish Cream or other
Irish cream liqueur

1 cup diced banana

½ cup diced orange

½ to ¾ cup vanilla ice cream

Place all ingredients in a blender, and mix by
using the on/off pulse function until the ingredients are mostly blended. Continue mixing,
gradually increasing the speed, just until the
mixture is smooth. Pour the smoothie into a
glass and garnish with an Almond Pirouette
(page 228), if desired. For an authentic touch,
serve the smoothie in a Cocktail glass.

Blue Velvet Smoothie

1 SERVING

2 tablespoons Midori or other melon liqueur

2 tablespoons raspberry liqueur

¾ cup diced cantaloupe

¾ cup raspberries

½ cup vanilla ice cream

¼ to ½ teaspoon blue curaçao

Place the melon liqueur, raspberry liqueur, cantaloupe, raspberries, and ice cream in a blender, and mix by using the on/off pulse function until the ingredients are mostly blended. Continue mixing, gradually increasing the speed, until the mixture is smooth. Pour the smoothie into a glass and float blue curaçao on top. Garnish with Berries on a Skewer (page 232), if desired. For an authentic touch, serve the smoothie in a Cocktail glass.

Cap Martin Smoothie

1 SERVING

2 tablespoons crème de cassis

1 tablespoon cognac (or brandy)

1 ½ cups diced pineapple

Place all ingredients in a blender, and mix by using the on/off pulse function until the ingredients are mostly blended. Continue mixing, gradually increasing the speed, until the mixture is smooth. Pour the smoothie into a glass and garnish the rim with an Orange Wheel (page 237), if desired. For an authentic touch, serve the smoothie in a Cocktail glass.

Chambord Royale Smoothie

1 SERVING

2 tablespoons Chambord or other raspberry
  liqueur

2 tablespoons vodka

1 tablespoon white cranberry juice

1 cup diced pineapple

½ cup raspberries

Place all ingredients in a blender, and mix by using the on/off pulse function until the ingredients are mostly blended. Continue mixing, gradually increasing the speed, until the mixture is smooth. Pour the smoothie into a glass and garnish with Berries on a Skewer (page 232), if desired. For an authentic touch, serve the smoothie in a Cocktail glass.

Creamsicle Smoothie

1 SERVING

1 ½ tablespoons Grand Marnier or other orange
   liqueur

1 tablespoon white crème de cacao

1 tablespoon Amaretto

1 ½ cups diced orange

½ cup vanilla ice cream

Place all ingredients in a blender, and mix by
using the on/off pulse function until the ingredients are mostly blended. Continue mixing,
gradually increasing the speed, until the mixture
is smooth. Pour the smoothie into a glass and
garnish with a Cinnamon and Sugar Twist (page
233), if desired. For an authentic touch, serve
the smoothie in a Cocktail glass.

Curacao Cooler Smoothie

1 SERVING

3 tablespoons blue curaçao

2 tablespoons light rum

1 teaspoon fresh lime juice

1 ½ cups diced orange

½ cup orange sorbet

Place all ingredients in a blender, and mix by using the on/off pulse function until the ingredients are mostly blended. Continue mixing, gradually increasing the speed, until the mixture is smooth. Pour the smoothie into a glass and garnish the rim with a Lime Wheel (page 237), if desired. For an authentic touch, serve the smoothie in a Collins glass.

Danish Snowball Smoothie

1 SERVING

3 tablespoons Cherry Heering or other cherry liqueur

1 ½ cups diced cherries

1 cup vanilla ice cream

Place all ingredients in a blender, and mix by using the on/off pulse function until the ingredients are mostly blended. Continue mixing, gradually increasing the speed, until the mixture is smooth. Pour the smoothie into a glass and garnish with an Almond Pirouette (page 238), if desired. For an authentic touch, serve the smoothie in a Wine glass.

Frangelico Colada Smoothie

1 SERVING

6 tablespoons Frangelico or other hazelnut liqueur

1 1/2 cups diced pineapple

1/2 to 3/4 cup coconut gelato or other coconut
(or vanilla) ice cream

Place all ingredients in a blender, and mix by
using the on/off pulse function until the ingredients are mostly blended. Continue mixing,
gradually increasing the speed, until the mixture
is smooth. Pour the smoothie into a glass and
garnish with an Almond Pirouette (page 228),
if desired. For an authentic touch, serve the
smoothie in a Collins glass.

Golden Cadillac Smoothie

1 SERVING

2 tablespoons Galliano

1 ½ tablespoons white crème de cacao

1 ½ cups diced orange

¾ cup vanilla ice cream

Place all ingredients in a blender, and mix by using the on/off pulse function until the ingredients are mostly blended. Continue mixing, gradually increasing the speed, until the mixture is smooth. Pour the smoothie into a glass and garnish with a Cinnamon and Sugar Twist (page 233), if desired. For an authentic touch, serve the smoothie in a Cocktail glass.

Golden Dream Smoothie

1 SERVING

3 tablespoons Galliano

2 tablespoons Cointreau, triple sec, or other orange liqueur

1 ½ cups diced orange

½ to ¾ cup vanilla ice cream

Place all ingredients in a blender, and mix by using the on/off pulse function until the ingredients are mostly blended. Continue mixing, gradually increasing the speed, until the mixture is smooth. Pour the smoothie into a glass and garnish the rim with an Orange, Lemon, and Cherry Combo (page 239), if desired. For an authentic touch, serve the smoothie in a Cocktail glass.

June Bug Smoothie

1 SERVING

1 to 1 ½ tablespoons Midori or other melon liqueur

1 to 1 ½ tablespoons peach liqueur

1 to 1 ½ tablespoons crème de banana or other banana liqueur

½ cup diced cantaloupe

½ cup diced peach

½ cup diced banana

Place all ingredients in a blender, and mix by using the on/off pulse function until the ingredients are mostly blended. Continue mixing, gradually increasing the speed, until the mixture is smooth. Pour the smoothie into a glass and garnish with Melon Balls on a Skewer (page 236), if desired. For an authentic touch, serve the smoothie in a Cocktail glass.

Kowloon Smoothie

1 SERVING

2 tablespoons Grand Marnier or other orange
   liqueur

2 tablespoons Kahlúa or other coffee liqueur

1 ½ cups diced orange

½ cup orange sorbet

Place all ingredients in a blender, and mix by using the on/off pulse function until the ingredients are mostly blended. Continue mixing, gradually increasing the speed, until the mixture is smooth. Pour the smoothie into a glass and garnish the rim with an Orange Wheel (page 237), if desired. For an authentic touch, serve the smoothie in a Wine glass.

Lights of Havana Smoothie

1 SERVING

2 tablespoons Midori liqueur or other melon liqueur

2 tablespoons coconut rum

1 tablespoon lemon-lime soda

½ cup diced pineapple

½ cup diced orange

½ cup diced cantaloupe

Place all ingredients in a blender, and mix by using the on/off pulse function until the ingredients are mostly blended. Continue mixing, gradually increasing the speed, until the mixture is smooth. Pour the smoothie into a glass and garnish the rim with a Pineapple Spear (page 245), if desired. For an authentic touch, serve the smoothie in a Collins glass.

Melon Cocktail Smoothie

1 SERVING

1 ½ tablespoons Midori or other melon liqueur

1 ½ tablespoons gin

1 tablespoon triple sec or other orange liqueur

1 ½ cups diced cantaloupe

¼ cup lemon sorbet

Place all ingredients in a blender, and mix by using the on/off pulse function until the ingredients are mostly blended. Continue mixing, gradually increasing the speed, until the mixture is smooth. Pour the smoothie into a glass and garnish with Melon Balls on a Skewer (page 236), if desired. For an authentic touch, serve the smoothie in a Cocktail glass.

Melon Cooler Smoothie

1 SERVING

2 tablespoons Midori or other melon liqueur

1 tablespoon peach Schnapps

1 tablespoon raspberry liqueur

½ cup diced cantaloupe

½ cup diced peach

½ cup diced pineapple

½ cup raspberry sorbet

Place all ingredients in a blender, and mix by using the on/off pulse function until the ingredients are mostly blended. Continue mixing, gradually increasing the speed, until the mixture is smooth. Pour the smoothie into a glass and garnish with Berries on a Skewer (page 232), if desired. For an authentic touch, serve the smoothie in a Cocktail glass.

Nutty Colada Smoothie

1 SERVING

1/4 cup Amaretto

2 tablespoons gold rum

1 1/2 cups diced pineapple

1/2 cup coconut gelato or other coconut (or vanilla) ice cream

Place all ingredients in a blender, and mix by using the on/off pulse function until the ingredients are mostly blended. Continue mixing, gradually increasing the speed, until the mixture is smooth. Pour the smoothie into a glass and garnish with a Pineapple Chip (page 243), if desired. For an authentic touch, serve the smoothie in a Collins glass.

Papaya Cream Smoothie

1 SERVING

2 tablespoons crème de cassis

1 ½ cups diced papaya (or mango)

½ cup vanilla ice cream

Place all ingredients in a blender, and mix by using the on/off pulse function until the ingredients are mostly blended. Continue mixing, gradually increasing the speed, until the mixture is smooth. Pour the smoothie into a glass and garnish with a Cinnamon and Sugar Twist (page 233), if desired. For an authentic touch, serve the smoothie in a Wine glass.

Peugeot Smoothie

1 SERVING

3 tablespoons Cointreau, triple sec, or other
   orange liqueur

1 ½ tablespoons Calvados or other apple liqueur

1 teaspoon Sugar Syrup (page 56), or to taste
   (optional)

1 cup diced orange

½ cup diced apple

½ cup orange sorbet

Place all ingredients in a blender, and mix by using the on/off pulse function until the ingredients are mostly blended. Continue mixing, gradually increasing the speed, until the mixture is smooth. Pour the smoothie into a glass and garnish with an Apple Chip (page 230), if desired. For an authentic touch, serve the smoothie in a Cocktail glass.

Raspberry Colada Smoothie

1 SERVING

1 ½ tablespoons Chambord or other raspberry
liqueur

1 ½ tablespoons light rum

1 cup diced pineapple

½ cup diced raspberries

½ cup coconut gelato or other coconut (or vanilla)
ice cream

Place all ingredients in a blender, and mix by
using the on/off pulse function until the ingredients are mostly blended. Continue mixing,
gradually increasing the speed, until the mixture
is smooth. Pour the smoothie into a glass and
garnish with Berries on a Skewer (page 232), if
desired. For an authentic touch, serve the
smoothie in a Cocktail glass.

Rive Gauche Smoothie

1 SERVING

2 tablespoons peach Schnapps

1 ½ tablespoons gin

1 ½ tablespoons Campari

1 ½ tablespoons Cointreau, triple sec, or other orange liqueur

1 ½ cups diced pineapple

Place all ingredients in a blender, and mix by using the on/off pulse function until the ingredients are mostly blended. Continue mixing, gradually increasing the speed, until the mixture is smooth. Pour the smoothie into a glass and garnish with a Pineapple Chip (page 243), if desired. For an authentic touch, serve the smoothie in a Cocktail glass.

Rolls Royce Smoothie

1 SERVING

2 tablespoons Cointreau, triple sec, or other
orange liqueur

2 tablespoons cognac (or brandy)

1 ½ cups diced orange

½ cup orange sorbet

Place all ingredients in a blender, and mix by using the on/off pulse function until the ingredients are mostly blended. Continue mixing, gradually increasing the speed, until the mixture is smooth. Pour the smoothie into a glass and garnish with a Pineapple Bow (page 242), if desired. For an authentic touch, serve the smoothie in a Cocktail glass.

Strawberry Storm Smoothie

1 SERVING

1 ½ tablespoons strawberry Schnapps or liqueur

1 tablespoon Kahlúa or other coffee liqueur

1 cup diced pineapple

½ cup diced strawberries

½ cup vanilla ice cream

Place all ingredients in a blender, and mix by using the on/off pulse function until the ingredients are mostly blended. Continue mixing, gradually increasing the speed, until the mixture is smooth. Pour the smoothie into a glass and garnish the rim with a Strawberry Fan (page 247), if desired. For an authentic touch, serve the smoothie in a Cocktail glass.

Tricycle Smoothie

1 SERVING

¼ cup triple sec or other orange liqueur

1 ½ cups diced orange

½ cup vanilla ice cream

Place all ingredients in a blender, and mix by using the on/off pulse function until the ingredients are mostly blended. Continue mixing, gradually increasing the speed, until the mixture is smooth. Pour the smoothie into a glass and garnish with an Almond Pirouette (page 228), if desired. For an authentic touch, serve the smoothie in a Wine glass.

Ultimate June Bug Smoothie

1 SERVING

2 tablespoons Midori or other melon liqueur

1 ½ tablespoons coconut rum

1 ½ tablespoons brandy

½ cup diced cantaloupe

½ cup diced pineapple

½ cup diced banana

2 tablespoons lemon sorbet

Place all ingredients in a blender, and mix by using the on/off pulse function until the ingredients are mostly blended. Continue mixing, gradually increasing the speed, until the mixture is smooth. Pour the smoothie into a glass and garnish with Melon Balls on a Skewer (page 236), if desired. For an authentic touch, serve the smoothie in a Cocktail glass.

CHAPTER 10

Champagne, Asti Spumante, and Wines

Sparkling and Otherwise

*I drink champagne when I win,
to celebrate . . . and I drink
champagne when I lose,
to console myself.*

—NAPOLEAN BONAPARTE

Asti Spumante is only one of a family of sparkling wines, the most renowned of which is champagne. While champagne is the premier choice for weddings, anniversaries, and toasts, its mellower cousin, Asti, is the preferred ingredient for embellishing a smoothie because of its sweet and fruity flavor.

Have you ever wondered about the night they invented champagne? Are you curious who "they" were? The simple answer is we don't know who "they" were, but we do know this bit of history: The first sparkling wine was developed in France in the sixteenth century. It is known that in the seventeenth century, the Benedictine monk Dom Pérignon, a cellar master at the Abbey of Hautvilliers in Epernay, France, developed the *Méthode Champenoise,* a process that continues to be used today to make a wide variety of the finest sparkling wines. The Dom's name still graces one of the most expensive brands of champagne.

Only sparkling wines made in the French district of Champagne can be legally labeled Champagne, leading wine makers of similar products in other European countries to christen their bubbly with different names and to endow them with distinctive taste characteristics. As confusing as Champagne (a sparkling wine from the French district) vs. champagne (pretenders from other locations) can sometimes be, the name *Asti Spumante* has its own esoteric origins. "Spumante" is the Italian word for "sparkling," while "Asti" is the name of a town in the Piedmont region of Italy. Wine makers from this town produce a sparkling wine called Asti Spumante, which is made from the very fragrant Muscat grapes grown in the region. Thus, the Italian sparkling wine, Asti Spumante, was born. While Asti Spumante is clearly one of the most popular sweet sparkling wines, similar products originating in other countries can also be useful as smoothie ingredients. For example, Cava is a

Spanish bubbly that comes from the Penedes area of Catalonia. In the United States, California and New York are the leading sparkling wine producers.

Other sweet, but not sparkling, wines—such as vermouth and sherry or an aperitif such as Campari—can be added to a cocktail smoothie with a wonderful flavor-enhancing effect. Naturally, the bubbles in Asti are lost when added to a smoothie, but it's the flavor of the liquor that is important in these recipes to mimic the combination of ingredients of their cocktail counterparts.

So, fill champagne glasses with Mimosa Smoothies made with your favorite sweet sparkling wine and oranges, and see if your guests exclaim, as did Dom Pérignon after his first taste of the magical beverage, "I am drinking stars!"

Barracuda Smoothie

1 SERVING

¼ cup (or more) Asti Spumante or other sweet
   sparkling wine

2 tablespoons gold rum

1 tablespoon Galliano

1 teaspoon Sugar Syrup (page 56), or to taste

½ teaspoon fresh lime juice

1½ cups diced pineapple

Place all ingredients in a blender, and mix by
using the on/off pulse function until the ingredients are mostly blended. Continue mixing,
gradually increasing the speed, until the mixture
is smooth. Pour the smoothie into a glass and
garnish with a maraschino cherry, if desired. For
an authentic touch, serve the smoothie in a hollowed-out pineapple shell.

Bellini "De Luxe" Smoothie

1 SERVING

¼ cup (or more) Asti Spumante or other sweet
   sparkling wine

1 ½ tablespoons cognac (or brandy)

1 ½ tablespoons peach liqueur

1 teaspoon Sugar Syrup (page 56), or to taste

1 ½ cups diced peach

¼ cup lemon sorbet

Place all ingredients in a blender, and mix by
using the on/off pulse function until the ingredients are mostly blended. Continue mixing,
gradually increasing the speed, until the mixture
is smooth. Pour the smoothie into a glass and
garnish the rim with an Orange, Lemon, and
Cherry Combo (page 239), if desired. For an
authentic touch, serve the smoothie in a Champagne glass.

Cadiz Smoothie

1 SERVING

1 ½ tablespoons medium dry amontillado sherry

1 ½ tablespoons blackberry liqueur

1 tablespoon triple sec or other orange liqueur

1 ½ cups blackberries

½ cup vanilla ice cream

Place all ingredients in a blender, and mix by using the on/off pulse function until the ingredients are mostly blended. Continue mixing, gradually increasing the speed, until the mixture is smooth. Pour the smoothie into a glass and garnish with Berries on a Skewer (page 232), if desired. For an authentic touch, serve the smoothie in an Old-Fashioned glass.

Flirtini Smoothie

1 SERVING

¼ cup Asti Spumante or other sweet
sparkling wine

1½ tablespoons vodka

1½ cups diced pineapple

Place all ingredients in a blender, and mix by
using the on/off pulse function until the ingredients are mostly blended. Continue mixing, gradually increasing the speed, until the mixture is
smooth. Pour the smoothie into a glass and garnish with a Pineapple Bow (page 242), if desired.
For an authentic touch, serve the smoothie in a
Champagne glass.

Mimosa Smoothie

1 SERVING

½ cup Asti Spumante or other sweet
  sparkling wine

1 to 2 teaspoons Sugar Syrup (page 56), or to
  taste (optional)

1 ½ cups diced orange

½ cup orange sorbet

Place all ingredients in a blender, and mix by
using the on/off pulse function until the ingredients are mostly blended. Continue mixing,
gradually increasing the speed, until the mixture
is smooth. Pour the smoothie into a glass and
garnish the rim with an Orange Wheel (page
237), if desired. For an authentic touch, serve
the smoothie in a Wine glass.

Nijinski Blinova Smoothie

1 SERVING

¹/₄ cup Asti Spumante or other sweet
   sparkling wine

2 tablespoons vodka

1 tablespoon peach Schnapps

1 teaspoon Sugar Syrup (page 56), or to taste
   (optional)

1 ¹/₂ cups diced peach

¹/₂ cup peach sorbet

Place all ingredients in a blender, and mix by
using the on/off pulse function until the ingredients are mostly blended. Continue mixing,
gradually increasing the speed, until the mixture
is smooth. Pour the smoothie into a glass and
garnish with a Mint Leaves (page 238), if desired. For an authentic touch, serve the
smoothie in a Champagne glass.

Pacific Palisades Smoothie

1 SERVING

¼ to ⅓ cup Asti Spumante or other sweet
    sparkling wine

3 tablespoons Campari

1 ½ cups diced orange

½ cup orange sorbet

Place all ingredients in a blender, and mix by
using the on/off pulse function until the ingredients
are mostly blended. Continue mixing,
gradually increasing the speed, until the mixture
is smooth. Pour the smoothie into a glass and
garnish the rim with an Orange Wheel (page
237), if desired. For an authentic touch, serve
the smoothie in a Wine glass.

Raymond Hitchcocktail Smoothie

1 SERVING

6 tablespoons sweet vermouth

1 cup diced orange

½ cup diced pineapple

½ cup orange sorbet

Place all ingredients in a blender, and mix by using the on/off pulse function until the ingredients are mostly blended. Continue mixing, gradually increasing the speed, until the mixture is smooth. Pour the smoothie into a glass and garnish the rim with a Pineapple Wedge (page 245), if desired. For an authentic touch, serve the smoothie in an Old-Fashioned glass.

Satin Whiskers Cocktail Smoothie

1 SERVING

2 tablespoons sweet vermouth

2 tablespoons dry vermouth

1 tablespoon gin

½ tablespoon Grand Marnier or other orange liqueur

1½ cups diced orange

½ cup orange sorbet

Place all ingredients in a blender, and mix by using the on/off pulse function until the ingredients are mostly blended. Continue mixing, gradually increasing the speed, until the mixture is smooth. Pour the smoothie into a glass and garnish the rim with an Orange Wheel (page 237), if desired. For an authentic touch, serve the smoothie in a Wine glass.

The Grand Screwdriver Smoothie

1 SERVING

¼ cup Asti Spumante or other sweet sparkling wine

2 tablespoons Grand Marnier or other orange liqueur

1½ cups diced orange

½ cup orange sorbet

Place all ingredients in a blender, and mix by using the on/off pulse function until the ingredients are mostly blended. Continue mixing, gradually increasing the speed, until the mixture is smooth. Pour the smoothie into a glass and garnish the rim with an Orange Wheel (page 237), if desired. For an authentic touch, serve the smoothie in a Champagne glass.

Yaka-Hula-Hicky-Dula Smoothie

1 SERVING

3 tablespoons dry vermouth

3 tablespoons dark rum

1 teaspoon Sugar Syrup (page 56), or to taste (optional)

1 ½ cups diced pineapple

Place all ingredients in a blender, and mix by using the on/off pulse function until the ingredients are mostly blended. Continue mixing, gradually increasing the speed, until the mixture is smooth. Pour the smoothie into a glass and garnish the rim with a Pineapple Chip (page 243), if desired. For an authentic touch, serve the smoothie in a Cocktail glass.

Yellow Rattler Smoothie

1 SERVING

2 tablespoons sweet vermouth

2 tablespoons dry vermouth

2 tablespoons gin

1 teaspoon Sugar Syrup (page 56), or to taste
   (optional)

1 ½ cups diced orange

½ cup orange sorbet

Place all ingredients in a blender, and mix by
using the on/off pulse function until the ingredients are mostly blended. Continue mixing,
gradually increasing the speed, until the mixture
is smooth. Pour the smoothie into a glass and
garnish the rim with an Orange Wheel (page
237), if desired. For an authentic touch, serve
the smoothie in a Wine glass.

CHAPTER

Brandy

Smoothies to Savor

*All alcoholic drinks, rightly used,
are good for body and soul alike,
but as a restorative of both
there is nothing like brandy.*

—GEORGE SAINTSBURY,
English journalist

Brandy (or distilled wine) is a strong alcoholic spirit distilled from a variety of fruits such as blackberries, apples, apricots, cherries, grapes, and peaches. When it is made from only grapes, the term *brandy,* alone, is used to describe the spirit. If it is distilled from any other fruit, it takes on the name of that ingredient as well.

Brandy made from peaches, for example, is called *peach brandy*.

The first use of concentrated wine was in ancient Greece, where it was used as an antiseptic or an anesthetic agent. The origin of brandy for use as a flavorful alcoholic drink can be traced back to medieval times. Before brandy was introduced, people were enjoying wines produced in high-quality vineyards in various regions throughout France. Dating as far back as the thirteenth century, these wines were shipped to Northern Europe and enjoyed by the English, Scandinavians, and Dutch. It was the northern Europeans' high demand for the wines of southern France that led to the accidental invention of brandy.

In the sixteenth century, Dutch traders came to the Cognac area to purchase the renowned wines from the Champagne and Borderies region to take back to Holland. How to transport large quantities of wine was of concern to these traders. If they could reduce the volume of the wine, it would be cheaper to transport. Another consideration was that the low alcohol wines would deteriorate during the long sea voyage back to Holland. The Dutch merchants set up stills in the Charente region and discovered that by double-distilling the wines, and lowering their water content (but not the alcohol), they could not only be reduced in volume but become better able to tolerate the long voyages. Another exciting revelation was uncovered when the concentrated wines arrived at their final destinations. The wine seemed to improve during the time required to transport and unload the wooden casks. Moreover, it was good enough to enjoy straight from the cask once it had aged.

In time, the stills installed by the Dutch were replaced by ones the French developed; and at the same time, they greatly improved the technique of double distillation. The rest is history.

While cognac is a brandy, not all brandies can be called cognac. Cognac is the most esteemed brandy in the world. It can only be made from St. Emilion *(or ugni blanc),* Colombard, or *folle blanche* grapes and distilled in the area surrounding the town of Cognac in the Charentes region of western France. The seven areas within this region include Grande Champagne and Petite Champagne, as well as Bois Ordinaires, Bois Communs, Fins Bois, Bons Bois, and Borderies. Cognac is always double distilled in small copper stills and then aged in oak casks for a minimum of two and a half years. Most cognacs age much longer, with the best aging 20 to 30 years. All cognacs are a blend of a variety of different spirits. In fact, a "VSOP" (see next paragraph) cognac can be the result of blending as many as 50 cognacs.

Because cognac is the most prestigious of all brandies, it is given stars and letters to signify its quality. The stars and letters are found on the labels and regulated by the French government. As an example, VO stands for "Very Old," which means that the cognac is at least four years old. You'll soon see, however, that the very best cognacs are much older. VS stands for "Very Superior" brandy that has aged a minimum of two years. XO is "Extra Old" and has aged a minimum of six years, while VSOP means "Very Superior Old Pale," indicating that the brandy has aged at least 10 years. Distillers also produce premium cognacs that are identified by terms such as "Napolean" or "Extra," which means they are quite old. The best cognacs are Courvoisier, Hennessy, Remy Martin, and Martell. Lesser-known cognacs to look for include Delamain, Monnet, Camus, and Hine, just to name a few.

Armagnac is France's other great brandy. It is distilled only once in a continuous copper still (cognac, you may remember, is distilled twice). The preferred Armagnac has aged between 15 and 25 years. This fine French brandy is produced in Gascony, which is located south of Cognac. The three main areas that produce Armagnac include Bas Aremagnac, Haut Armagnac, and Tenareze. The grapes that are most often used are the Colombard, Baco, Folle Balanche, and Ugni Blanc.

While the French are famous for their brandy, it is also produced in other countries such as Spain, Portugal, South Africa, Germany, Italy, Greece, and Australia. Interestingly, in terms of pure volume, Spain is the leading producer of brandy. Brandy is also made in the United States, with more than 95 percent of production occurring in California.

There is a significant difference in price between the finest brandies and the more ordinary varieties. While you may want to serve a finer brandy for after-dinner sipping, a less expensive version will satisfy most tastes when used as a smoothie ingredient.

As you can see, the basic joys of sipping a good cognac have not changed much in the last 900 years, but now it's time for this ancient delight to reinvent itself in a 21st-century way. So, fill your favorite cocktail glass with a Brandy Alexander Smoothie and wish your partner *"A votre santé!"* To your health!

American Beauty Smoothie

1 SERVING

2 tablespoons cognac (or brandy)

2 tablespoons dry vermouth

1 teaspoon grenadine

Dash of crème de menthe

1 ½ cups diced orange

½ cup orange sorbet

Place all ingredients in a blender, and mix by using the on/off pulse function until the ingredients are mostly blended. Continue mixing, gradually increasing the speed, until the mixture is smooth. Pour the smoothie into a glass and garnish with Mint Leaves (page 238), if desired. For an authentic touch, serve the smoothie in a Cocktail glass.

Belmont Park Smoothie

1 SERVING

2 tablespoons apple brandy

2 tablespoons apricot brandy

1 tablespoon gin

1 teaspoon Sugar Syrup (see page 56), or to taste

1 1/2 cups diced apricots

1/2 cup orange sorbet

1/2 teaspoon grenadine

Place the apple brandy, apricot brandy, gin, Sugar Syrup, apricots, and sorbet in a blender, and mix by using the on/off pulse function until the ingredients are mostly blended. Continue mixing, gradually increasing the speed, until the mixture is smooth. Pour the smoothie into a glass and float grenadine on top. Garnish with an Apple Chip (page 230), if desired. For an authentic touch, serve the smoothie in a Cocktail glass.

Between the Sheets Smoothie

1 SERVING

3 tablespoons cognac (or brandy)

2 tablespoons light rum

1 tablespoon triple sec or other orange liqueur

1 ½ cups diced orange

¼ cup lemon sorbet

Place all ingredients in a blender, and mix by using the on/off pulse function until the ingredients are mostly blended. Continue mixing, gradually increasing the speed, until the mixture is smooth. Pour the smoothie into a glass and garnish the rim with an Orange, Lemon, and Cherry Combo (page 239), if desired. For an authentic touch, serve the smoothie in a Cocktail glass.

Blackjack Smoothie

1 SERVING

2 tablespoons blackberry brandy

2 tablespoons brandy

1 ½ cups blackberries

¾ cup vanilla ice cream

Place all ingredients in a blender, and mix by using the on/off pulse function until the ingredients are mostly blended. Continue mixing, gradually increasing the speed, until the mixture is smooth. Pour the smoothie into a glass and garnish with Berries on a Skewer (page 232), if desired. For an authentic touch, serve the smoothie in a Cocktail glass.

Brandy Alexander Smoothie

1 SERVING

3 tablespoons brandy

2 tablespoons crème de cacao

¾ cup diced banana

¾ cup diced pineapple

1 cup vanilla ice cream

Place all ingredients in a blender, and mix by using the on/off pulse function until the ingredients are mostly blended. Continue mixing, gradually increasing the speed, until the mixture is smooth. Pour the smoothie into a glass and garnish with a Cinnamon and Sugar Twist (page 233), if desired. For an authentic touch, serve the smoothie in a Cocktail glass.

Brandy Melba Smoothie

1 SERVING

3 tablespoons brandy

1 tablespoon peach Schnapps

1 tablespoon raspberry liqueur

1 cup diced peach

1/2 cup raspberries

1/2 cup peach or raspberry sorbet

Place all ingredients in a blender, and mix by using the on/off pulse function until the ingredients are mostly blended. Continue mixing, gradually increasing the speed, until the mixture is smooth. Pour the smoothie into a glass and garnish with Berries on a Skewer (page 232), if desired. For an authentic touch, serve the smoothie in a Cocktail glass.

California Dreaming Smoothie

1 SERVING

¼ cup apricot brandy

1 cup diced orange

½ cup diced apricots

½ cup orange sorbet

Place all ingredients in a blender, and mix by using the on/off pulse function until the ingredients are mostly blended. Continue mixing, gradually increasing the speed, until the mixture is smooth. Pour the smoothie into a glass and garnish the rim with an Orange Wheel (page 237), if desired. For an authentic touch, serve the smoothie in a Parfait glass.

East India Cocktail Smoothie

1 SERVING

3 tablespoons brandy

1 teaspoon dark rum

1/2 teaspoon triple sec or other orange liqueur

1 teaspoon Sugar Syrup (page 56), or to taste
   (optional)

1 1/2 cups diced pineapple

Place all ingredients in a blender, and mix by using the on/off pulse function until the ingredients are mostly blended. Continue mixing, gradually increasing the speed, until the mixture is smooth. Pour the smoothie into a glass and garnish the rim with a Pineapple Spear (page 245), if desired. For an authentic touch, serve the smoothie in a Cocktail glass.

Fuzzy Brother Smoothie

1 SERVING

3 tablespoons brandy

1 tablespoon peach Schnapps

1 cup diced orange

½ cup diced peach

½ cup peach sorbet

Place all ingredients in a blender, and mix by using the on/off pulse function until the ingredients are mostly blended. Continue mixing, gradually increasing the speed, until the mixture is smooth. Pour the smoothie into a glass and garnish with a Fruit Skewer (page 236), if desired. For an authentic touch, serve the smoothie in an Old-Fashioned glass.

Georgia Peach Smoothie

1 SERVING

3 tablespoons brandy

1 tablespoon peach brandy

1 tablespoon club soda

1 teaspoon crème de banana or other banana liqueur

1 teaspoon Sugar Syrup (page 56), or to taste

¾ cup diced peach

¾ cup diced banana

Place all ingredients in a blender, and mix by using the on/off pulse function until the ingredients are mostly blended. Continue mixing, gradually increasing the speed, until the mixture is smooth. Pour the smoothie into a glass and garnish with a Crisp Banana Wafer (page 235), if desired. For an authentic touch, serve the smoothie in a Cocktail glass.

Golf El Paraiso Smoothie

1 SERVING

1 ½ tablespoons apple brandy

1 ½ tablespoons light rum

1 teaspoon grenadine

1 cup diced orange

½ cup diced apple

½ cup orange sorbet

2 tablespoons lemon sorbet

Place all ingredients in a blender, and mix by using the on/off pulse function until the ingredients are mostly blended. Continue mixing, gradually increasing the speed, until the mixture is smooth. Pour the smoothie into a glass and garnish with an Apple Chip (page 230), if desired. For an authentic touch, serve the smoothie in an Old-Fashioned glass.

La Jolla Smoothie

1 SERVING

3 tablespoons brandy

1 tablespoon crème de banana or other banana liqueur

1 cup diced orange

½ cup diced banana

½ cup orange sorbet

2 tablespoons lemon sorbet

Place all ingredients in a blender, and mix by using the on/off pulse function until the ingredients are mostly blended. Continue mixing, gradually increasing the speed, until the mixture is smooth. Pour the smoothie into a glass and garnish the rim with an Orange, Lemon, and Cherry Combo (page 239), if desired. For an authentic touch, serve the smoothie in a Cocktail glass.

Millennium Cocktail Smoothie

1 SERVING

3 tablespoons Courvoisier cognac (or brandy)

1 ½ tablespoons curaçao

1 ½ cups diced pineapple

½ cup orange sorbet

Place all ingredients in a blender, and mix by using the on/off pulse function until the ingredients are mostly blended. Continue mixing, gradually increasing the speed, until the mixture is smooth. Pour the smoothie into a glass and garnish with a Pineapple Bow (page 242), if desired. For an authentic touch, serve the smoothie in a Cocktail glass.

Olympic Smoothie

1 SERVING

2 tablespoons cognac (or brandy)

2 tablespoons curaçao

1 ½ cups diced orange

½ cup orange sorbet

Place all ingredients in a blender, and mix by using the on/off pulse function until the ingredients are mostly blended. Continue mixing, gradually increasing the speed, until the mixture is smooth. Pour the smoothie into a glass and garnish the rim with an Orange Wheel (page 237), if desired. For an authentic touch, serve the smoothie in a Cocktail glass.

Peach Fuzz Smoothie

1 SERVING

3 tablespoons peach brandy

1 tablespoon white crème de cacao

1 ½ cups diced peach

½ cup vanilla ice cream

1 teaspoon apple Schnapps

Place the peach brandy, crème de cacao, peach, and ice cream in a blender, and mix by using the on/off pulse function until the ingredients are mostly blended. Continue mixing, gradually increasing the speed, until the mixture is smooth. Pour the smoothie into a glass and float apple Schnapps on top. Garnish with an Apple Chip (page 230), if desired. For an authentic touch, serve the smoothie in a Cocktail glass.

Sidecar Smoothie

1 SERVING

2 tablespoons cognac (or brandy)

2 tablespoons Cointreau, triple sec, or other orange liqueur

1 ½ cups diced orange

2 tablespoons lemon sorbet

Place all ingredients in a blender, and mix by using the on/off pulse function until the ingredients are mostly blended. Continue mixing, gradually increasing the speed, until the mixture is smooth. Pour the smoothie into a glass and garnish the rim with an Orange, Lemon, and Cherry Combo (page 239), if desired. For an authentic touch, serve the smoothie in a Cocktail glass.

Strawberry Alexander Smoothie

1 SERVING

2 tablespoons brandy

2 tablespoons white crème de cacao

1 1/2 cups diced strawberries

1/2 to 3/4 cup vanilla ice cream

Place all ingredients in a blender, and mix by using the on/off pulse function until the ingredients are mostly blended. Continue mixing, gradually increasing the speed, until the mixture is smooth. Pour the smoothie into a glass and garnish the rim with a Strawberry Fan (page 247), if desired. For an authentic touch, serve the smoothie in a Cocktail glass.

Whitehall Club Smoothie

1 SERVING

2 tablespoons brandy

1 tablespoon gin

1 tablespoon Grand Marnier or other orange
   liqueur

1 teaspoon Sugar Syrup (page 56), or to taste

1 ½ cups diced orange

¼ cup lemon sorbet

½ teaspoon raspberry syrup

Place the brandy, gin, orange liqueur, Sugar
Syrup, orange, and sorbet in a blender, and mix
by using the on/off pulse function until the ingredients are mostly blended. Continue mixing,
gradually increasing the speed, until the mixture is
smooth. Pour the smoothie into a glass and float
raspberry syrup on top. Garnish with Berries on a
Skewer (page 232), if desired. For an authentic
touch, serve the smoothie in a Parfait glass.

CHAPTER 12

Garnishes for Tipsy Smoothies

✦

*Garnishes must be matched
like a tie to a suit.*

—FERAND POINT,
Ma Gastronomie

Smoothies are usually known for their unique combination of flavors and textures rather than for their appearance. However, by choosing the right garnish, you can magically create something visually grand out of otherwise simple ingredients, and transform an ordinary smoothie into an extraordinary cocktail. Whether you garnish your tipsy smoothie with something basic (such as an Orange Wheel) or more elaborate (a

Pineapple Chip, for example), the colors and shapes can create a cocktail that is striking in appearance. What's more, all the garnishes described in this chapter are exceptionally delicious.

In this chapter you will find a host of novel ideas for creating garnishes to dress up a tipsy smoothie. Most are not complicated to make, and many can be prepared well in advance—even frozen so you have a ready supply for an instant smoothie celebration. On the other hand, if you don't have the time or inclination to make your own garnishes, consider picking up fun accessories at your neighborhood party store, such as multi-colored and uniquely shaped straws, cocktail umbrellas, brightly colored metallic sparklers, paper flowers, or fancy swizzle sticks. In addition, a number of edible accessories are available on the Internet, such as Cookie Straws that are lined with chocolate and flavored with vanilla or strawberry, and Cookie Spoons made of edible cookies, which can be purchased plain or chocolate dipped (available at www.coffeeshoppe.net).

It's true that tipsy smoothies are inherently appealing, yet I'm convinced that once you've served one artfully decorated with a colorful, tasty embellishment, you'll agree that this touch not only showcases the cocktail but makes it seductively exciting.

Almond Pirouettes

Garnishing with an Almond Pirouette cookie is a delicious way to adorn many smoothies. Although a host of commercially made pirouettes are available in assorted sizes and flavors, I prefer to make my own.

6 PIROUETTES

3 tablespoons unbleached flour

2 tablespoons toasted almond flour*

2 tablespoons unsalted butter, at room temperature

1/4 cup powdered sugar

1 large egg white, beaten until foamy

1/4 teaspoon pure vanilla extract

Preheat oven to 350 degrees F. Line a baking sheet with parchment paper or a silicone mat. Set aside.

Combine the unbleached flour and toasted almond flour in a small bowl and blend well.

Place the butter and powdered sugar in a medium bowl, and beat with a hand-held electric mixer on medium speed for one minute or until well combined. Add half the flour mixture and beat on low speed until blended. Add the egg white and remaining flour mixture and beat just until incorporated. Add the vanilla and beat until smooth.

Spoon 1½ tablespoons of batter on each half of the prepared baking sheet. Spread the batter with the back of a spoon into a 6-inch circle, making sure the batter is thin but not transparent. (Don't worry if the batter looks uneven; it will even out during the baking process.) Bake for six to eight minutes, or until the edges begin to turn golden brown.

Allow the cookies to cool for one minute, and then use a metal spatula to loosen and quickly roll up the cookie into a tight cylinder or cigar shape. Place the cookies, seam side down, on a cake rack to cool completely. Allow the baking sheet to cool before repeating the process with the remaining batter. The cookies can be stored in an airtight container for up to three to five days, or frozen for a couple of weeks.

---

* Purchase toasted almond flour at King Arthur Flour, Norwich, VT; (800) 827-6836, or from The Bakers Catalogue Online, at www.kingarthurflour.com. If almond flour isn't available, simply use regular flour.

Apple Chips

Apple chips are crunchy, paper-thin slices of apples. They are the perfect garnish to dress up any smoothie. They add a sophisticated elegance to smoothies or other desserts, and are delicious as well. The chips are best when the apples are thinly sliced with a mandoline (a gourmet kitchen tool that uniformly slices fruits or vegetables) or vegetable slicer; however, with a little patience, you can use a sharp knife effectively.

16 TO 20 CHIPS

1 Granny Smith or Golden Delicious apple, unpeeled and uncored

4 cups cold water

¼ cup fresh lemon juice

2 cups granulated sugar

Preheat oven to 200 degrees F. Line a baking sheet with parchment paper or a silicone baking mat. Set aside.

Thinly slice the apples into horizontal rings, about $\frac{1}{16}$-inch thick. Place the apple rings in a bowl filled with 2 cups water and 2 tablespoons lemon juice. Set aside.

Combine the remaining 2 cups water and 2 tablespoons lemon juice, and the sugar in a large saucepan over medium-high heat. Cook for three to four minutes or until the mixture comes to a boil, stirring frequently to dissolve the sugar. Add the apples and cook for one to two minutes, or until the mixture returns to a boil.

Using tongs, remove the apples from the syrup and place them in a single layer on the prepared baking sheet. Pat excess syrup from the apples with a double layer of paper towels. Bake for one hour or until the apples are dry and crisp. If the apples are not crisp after an hour, turn off the oven and allow them to dry in the oven. The apple chips can be stored in an airtight container for up to three days.

Berries on a Skewer

This beautiful yet easy-to-prepare garnish adds rich color to most smoothies.

2 SKEWERS

½ cup fresh raspberries, blueberries, blackberries, or cranberries

2 wooden skewers, 6 to 10 inches long

Thread five to six berries of your choice onto the upper half of each skewer.

Cinnamon and Sugar Twists

For a whimsical and delicious touch, insert one or two cinnamon and sugar twists upright in a smoothie. These delectable twists, if made in advance and stored in the freezer, can be served directly without thawing and are equally as delicious when served at room temperature.

14 TWISTS

3 tablespoons granulated sugar

$1/4$ teaspoon ground cinnamon

$1/4$ box (or 4 ounces) Pepperidge Farm Pastry sheets

Flour, for dusting

1 small egg white, beaten until foamy

Combine the sugar and cinnamon in a small bowl and blend well. Set aside. Place two baking sheets on top of each other and line the top one with parchment paper. Set aside.

Remove one portion of pastry sheet and cut in half. (Rewrap the remaining half and return to box and freeze.) Wrap the pastry sheet in plastic wrap and allow it to sit at room temperature for 30 minutes.

Lightly dust a sheet of parchment paper with flour. Unfold the thawed pastry sheet (it should measure approximately $3\frac{1}{2}$ by 5 inches) and place it on the paper. Turn to coat both sides in the flour. Refold the pastry sheet (it should now measure 5 by 9½ inches) and place a piece of parchment paper on top. Using a rolling pin, flatten the pastry sheet into a 6-inch square (it does not have to be exact).

Brush the bottom half lightly with beaten egg white and sprinkle the cinnamon-sugar mixture over the egg white within ½-inch of the edges. Fold the top half (or side without any egg white and cinnamon-sugar) over and press the edges together. Place a piece of parchment paper on top of pastry sheet and roll it into an 8- by 10-inch rectangle. Leave the parchment on top of pastry sheet and refrigerate for one hour.

Preheat oven to 375 degrees F. When the pastry sheet is firm, remove the parchment paper. Using a pizza cutter or sharp knife, cut the sheet crosswise into ¼-inch strips. Working with one strip at a time, start in the center and work toward the end, twisting the ends of the dough strip in opposite directions until it looks like a long spiral. Trim the ends. Place each strip on the baking sheet, 1 inch apart. Press the ends down slightly to prevent the twists from curling up. Bake for 17 to 20 minutes or until golden brown. Remove the baking sheet from the oven and place it on a cooling rack. After five minutes, loosen the twists from the sheet. When the cinnamon and sugar twists are cool, they can be stored in an airtight container or resealable plastic bag in the freezer for several weeks, or at room temperature for up to one week.

Crisp Banana Wafers

These crispy wafers are simply made of puréed bananas that have been baked slowly in an oven until the mixture becomes brown and crisp. When cool, they are broken into irregular pieces that can be used to adorn any of the smoothies found in this book.

12 TO 16 WAFERS

2 medium bananas, cut into 1-inch pieces

1 to 2 tablespoons granulated sugar

Preheat oven to 200 degrees F. Line a baking sheet with a silicone baking mat. Set aside.

Place the bananas and sugar in the work bowl of a food processor fitted with a metal blade (or in a blender), and process for 45 seconds or until the bananas are puréed. Spoon the puréed bananas in the center of the prepared baking sheet. Using a metal spatula, spread the purée evenly into a rectangular shape, about ¹⁄₁₆-inch thick. The layer should almost cover the mat. Bake the banana purée for two and a half to three hours or until brown and completely dry. Remove the pan from the oven, place another baking sheet over the baked banana, and invert the pan. Gently remove the silicone pad and allow the baked banana to cool for 30 minutes to an hour. When cool, break the baked banana into irregular triangular shapes. The crisp banana wafers can be stored in an airtight container for up to three days.

Fruit Skewers

Fruit skewers make an attractive smoothie garnish when inserted into a tall glass. What's more, the fruit is a delicious complement to the smoothie. The combination and arrangement of fruits chosen from the list below is almost infinite. Also, keep in mind that even a skewer containing a single fruit, such as melon balls, can be as lovely as one made with a variety.

2 SKEWERS

2 grapes

2 kiwi slices, peeled and cut 1 inch thick

2 banana slices, peeled and cut 1 inch thick

2 pineapple cubes

2 melon balls

2 strawberries

2 stemless maraschino cherries

2 starfruit, cut 1/2 inch thick

2 wooden skewers, 6 to 10 inches long

Alternately thread different fruit pieces onto the upper half of the skewers, ending with the strawberry sitting on the top. Be sure to use skewers that are long enough to allow the bottom piece of fruit to rest comfortably on the rim of the glass. The fruit skewers can be kept refrigerated in an airtight container for up to two hours. (If using bananas, toss the slices in a little lemon juice to prevent them from turning brown.)

Lemon, Lime, and Orange Wheels

If you are fortunate enough to have a garnishing set that includes a food decorator tool or cannelure knife, follow the instructions given. If neither tool is available, you can use a fork and follow the simple technique my mother taught me for making fruit wheels.

5 TO 6 WHEELS

1 lemon, lime, or orange

Using a fork, start at one end of the fruit, and move the fork down to the other end, slightly piercing the skin with the fork tines. Repeat this process around the entire fruit until it appears vertically striped. Remove the ends and cut the fruit into ¼-inch-thick slices.

To hang the wheel over the rim of a glass, make a slit by cutting through the peel and halfway through the flesh. Fit the slit over the rim of the glass.

Mint Leaves

Mint leaves make an attractive accent when used to garnish a smoothie. The trick is to keep the leaves crisp.

1 BUNCH LEAVES

1 bunch mint leaves

Remove any rubber bands first. Next, cut off the root ends and lower part of the stems because they draw moisture from the fragile leaves. Once trimmed, loosely wrap the mint in a damp paper towel and place it in a large enough plastic bag so the leaves and stems will not be crushed. Place the mint on the top shelf of your refrigerator and use it within a few days. If the mint needs washing before use, simply immerse it in a bowl filled with cold water and swish it around with your hands. Scoop it up and gently blot dry with a paper towel or spin it in a salad spinner.

Orange, Lemon, and Cherry Combo

This spectacular colorful fruit combo dresses up any smoothie cocktail when it is placed on the rim of the glass.

2 COMBOS

2 orange slices, each with skin and cut
   ¼ inch thick

2 lemon slices, each with skin and cut
   ¼ inch thick

4 mint leaves (optional)

2 stemless maraschino cherries

Make a slit by cutting through the peel and halfway through the flesh of the orange and lemon slice. If using mint, place two mint leaves in each hole of the cherry where the pit was removed (if pit remains, cut a small slit in the top). Cut a slit on the opposite side of the cherry. Using the slits cut in each fruit, place an orange slice, followed by a lemon, and then a cherry on the rim of each glass.

Pear Chips

Like their apple and pineapple cousins, pear chips are crunchy, paper-thin slices of tantalizing flavor. They add a sophisticated elegance to smoothies, as well as other desserts. The chips are best when the pears are thinly sliced with a mandoline or vegetable slicer; however, with a little patience, you can make a sharp knife work effectively.

10 TO 12 CHIPS

2 cups cold water

1 cup granulated sugar

1 firm Bosc or red pear, unpeeled and uncored

Combine the water and sugar in a large saucepan over medium-high heat, and cook until the mixture comes to a boil, stirring frequently to dissolve the sugar.

Meanwhile, use a mandoline to thinly slice the pears into lengthwise slices, about ¹⁄₁₆ inch thick (or as thin as possible). Reduce the heat to low and add the pears, one slice at a time, to the water and sugar mixture. Cook for 10 minutes, or until the pears are transparent. Remove the saucepan from the heat and allow the pears to cool in the syrup.

Preheat oven to 275 degrees F. Line a baking sheet with parchment paper or a silicone baking mat. Set aside.

Using tongs, remove the pears from the syrup and place them in a single layer on the prepared baking sheet. Pat the pears dry with a double layer of paper towels. Bake for 30 to 40 minutes or until the pears are dry and crisp. (To test for doneness, remove a pear slice and allow it to cool. If it is not crisp, then bake the pears a little longer, and test again for crispness.) The pear chips can be stored in an airtight container for up to three days.

Pineapple Bows

Smoothies go uptown when garnished with this colorful and tasty pineapple bow tie.

4 BOWS

1 pineapple, base and spiny leaves removed

4 stemless maraschino cherries

4 wooden skewers, 10 inches long

Slice the pineapple (with its rind) into ½-inch-thick slices. Cut one slice into eight equally sized triangular segments. (Extra pineapple can be cut into cubes and placed in the freezer to be made into a smoothie.)

Thread one pineapple segment, rind side down, onto the upper half of a skewer. Thread a cherry on the skewer so it rests on the point of the pineapple segment. Thread another pineapple segment, point side down, so the tip rests on the cherry. Push the fruit to the top of the skewer, but be sure the skewer is not poking out of the top pineapple segment. Store the pineapple bows in an airtight container for up to two hours.

Pineapple Chips

This garnish can elevate pineapple smoothies, and many others, to a new dimension. The chips are deliciously sweet and look sensational when inserted upright into a smoothie. This is also a perfect garnish for a dish of sorbet or ice cream.

12 TO 18 CHIPS

1 fresh pineapple with top, base, sides (rind), and core removed

1 cup granulated sugar

1 cup cold water

Preheat oven to 225 degrees F. Line a baking sheet with a silicone mat. Set aside.

Using a mandoline or vegetable slicer if available, thinly slice the pineapple into horizontal rings, about 1/16-inch thick. (With patience, you can slice the pineapple rings with a knife.) Place the pineapple rings in a shallow roasting pan. Set aside.

Combine the sugar and water together in a small, heavy saucepan over moderate heat, and bring to a boil, stirring occasionally. Pour the hot mixture over the pineapple rings, and cover the pan with aluminum foil.

Place the pan over two stove burners; cook over low heat for 15 minutes. Remove the pan from the burners, allowing the pineapple rings to cool to room temperature.

Using tongs, remove the pineapple rings from the syrup and place them in a single layer on the prepared baking sheet. Bake for 60 to 90 minutes or until they turn golden brown. As soon as the pineapple chips are baked, they can be kept whole, formed into a rolled cigar shape, or cut into wedges. Allow the pineapple chips to cool before storing them in an airtight container for up to two days. The pineapple chips will become crisp as they cool.

Note: The pineapple chips can also be made by thinly slicing the pineapple into rings and placing them on a double thickness of paper towels. Pat the tops of each pineapple ring with paper towels, and then transfer them to a baking sheet lined with a silicone mat. Sprinkle ¼ teaspoon granulated sugar over each ring, and bake in a preheated oven at 350 degrees F for 60 to 90 minutes or until golden brown.

Pineapple Spears, Wedges, and Slices

Pineapple spears, wedges, or slices perched on the rim of a glass add a tasty, tropical flair to a smoothie. To be certain to get the sweetest part of the pineapple, use the section closest to the top, near the spiny leaves. Consider leaving the outside rind on the pineapple for added color.

4 SPEARS, WEDGES, OR SLICES

1 small pineapple

To make the pineapple spears, cut the pineapple in half, lengthwise, starting at the leafy end. Cut the resulting half lengthwise into four equal parts, beginning at the leafy end. Starting at the base of each of the four pieces, use a sharp knife to create a 2-inch slit, midway between the cut surface and the rind. Place the pineapple spear on the rim of the glass. (The remaining pineapple can be cut into cubes and placed in the freezer to be made into a smoothie.)

To make pineapple wedges, place the whole pineapple on its side and cut into ½-inch-thick slices; cut each slice in half. Each of the two pieces should now be in the shape of a half circle. Slice each half circle as though it was half a pie into three to four equal triangular pieces. Starting at the center, make a slit by cutting through the rind and halfway into the pineapple wedge. Fit the slit over the rim of the glass.

To make the pineapple slices, place the whole pineapple on its side and cut into ½-inch thick slices; cut each slice in half. Starting at the center, make a slit by cutting through the rind and halfway into the pineapple. Fit the slit over the rim of the glass.

Strawberry Fans

Strawberry Fans add a nice touch of color when placed on the rim of a glass, and are also a tasty treat.

2 FANS

2 whole firm strawberries, unhulled

Using a very sharp knife, make vertical cuts through the strawberry, starting ¼-inch down from the stem end and cutting through to the pointed end. Make about five to six very thin cuts, depending on the size of the strawberry. Place the strawberry on a plate and carefully spread the slices apart to resemble an opened fan. Slip a strawberry fan over the rim of each glass.

Index

International Conversion Chart

These are not exact equivalents: they have been slightly rounded to make measuring easier.

Liquid Measurements

American	Imperial	Metric	Australian
2 tablespoons (1 oz.)	1 fl. oz.	30 ml	1 tablespoon
¼ cup (2 oz.)	2 fl. oz.	60 ml	2 tablespoons
⅓ cup (3 oz.)	3 fl. oz.	80 ml	¼ cup
½ cup (4 oz.)	4 fl. oz.	125 ml	⅓ cup
⅔ cup (5 oz.)	5 fl. oz.	165 ml	½ cup
¾ cup (6 oz.)	6 fl. oz.	185 ml	⅔ cup
1 cup (8 oz.)	8 fl. oz.	250 ml	¾ cup

Spoon Measurements

American	Metric
¼ teaspoon	1 ml
½ teaspoon	2 ml
1 teaspoon	5 ml
1 tablespoon	15 ml

Weights

US/UK	Metric
1 oz.	30 grams (g)
2 oz.	60 g
4 oz. (¼ lb)	125 g
5 oz. (⅓ lb)	155 g
6 oz.	185 g
7 oz.	220 g
8 oz. (½ lb)	250 g
10 oz.	315 g
12 oz. (¾ lb)	375 g
14 oz.	440 g
16 oz. (1 lb)	500 g
2 lbs	1 kg

Oven Temperatures

Farenheit	Centigrade	Gas
250	120	½
300	150	2
325	160	3
350	180	4
375	190	5
400	200	6
450	230	8